River Guides of the Miramichi

Other Books by Wayne Curtis

Currents in the Stream
One Indian Summer
Fishing the Miramichi

River Guides
of the
Miramichi

WAYNE CURTIS

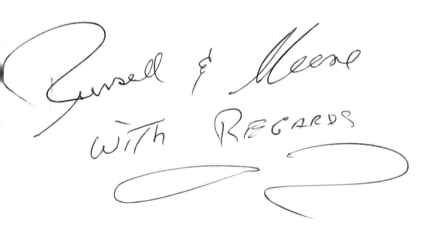

Russell & Neere
With REGARDS

GOOSE LANE

Published by Goose Lane Editions with the assistance of the Canada Council, the Department of Canadian Heritage, and the New Brunswick Department of Municipalities, Culture and Housing, 1997.

Edited by Laurel Boone and Rhona Sawlor.
Cover photo © Thomas R. Pero. Reproduced with permission. From left to right: Harold Gilks, Evelock Gilks and Winston Gilks.
Map detail of the Miramichi courtesy of the New Brunswick Crown Land Office, c 1945.
Page layout by Darren Lee, LEE~CURRENT Design.
Cover design by Julie Scriver and Darren Lee.
Printed in Canada by Gagné Printing.
10 9 8 7 6 5 4 3

Canadian Cataloguing in Publication Data

Curtis, Wayne, 1945-

    River guides of the Miramichi
    ISBN 0-86492-224-8

1. Fishing guides — New Brunswick — Miramichi River — Biography.
2. Fishing — New Brunswick — Miramichi River. I. Title.

SH414.C87 1997   799.1'1'092   C97-950040-0

Goose Lane Editions
469 King Street
Fredericton, New Brunswick
CANADA E3B 1E5

For Winston

Table of Contents

ACKNOWLEDGEMENTS XI

GUIDES AND GUESTS 13
THE GUIDE 23
ROY CURTIS 27
JACK JARDINE 33
PERCY MOUNTAIN 39
JOHN BROPHY 47
PAT BROPHY 53
THE GUIDES OF CHARLIE WADE'S CAMP 61
GUIDING JIM LORENTZ 65
JIM COLFORD 71
GORDON MUNN 75
CLAYTON FORAN 81
EUGENE HARRIS 85
ERNEST J. LONG 93
LLOYD WAUGH 101
MAX GILLESPIE 107
GUY SILLIKER 113
RALPH WARREN 123

John Curtis 127

Vincent Swazey 137

Renate Bullock 143

Bill MacKay 147

Mervin Green 153

Clayton Arthur Stewart 159

Merlin Palmer 163

Evelock Gilks 169

Guiding Gene Hill 173

Index 179

The Guide's Oath of Office

I do solemnly swear that I will faithfully perform the several duties of a guide under the Fish and Wildlife Act and Regulations. That I will especially endeavour to prevent the illegal taking of fish or wildlife and that I personally will adhere to the provisions of the Fish and Wildlife Act and the Regulations and all other game and fishery Acts applicable to the Province without fear, favour or affection. So help me God.

Acknowledgements

There are a number of Curtises mentioned in *River Guides of the Miramichi* who are not related to me at all or who may be distant cousins. Curtis is an old Miramichi name, and, like the MacDonalds in Cape Breton, the Curtis families have mingled the Scottish, English, and Irish backgrounds of our ancestors. However, I have featured John Curtis, who is my father, because, like the other guides in this book, and like his own father, he has spent a lifetime on this river. I also mention my two sons, Jeff and Jason Curtis, who have followed their father, grandfather, and great-grandfather into the profession of guiding. This part of my family history helps to explain why I wrote this book and why the guides I write about were so willing to talk to me.

I would like to thank the people who helped in the collecting of the material in this book. The river guides and their spouses who welcomed me into their homes for interviews deserve a special thanks. Without them this book would not have been possible. I also thank the guests whose names appear in the book and who were guided either by myself or by the other guides. I would like to thank Gene Hill and Jim Lorentz for letting me use them as examples of people I've worked with on the river. I am grateful to Tom Fuller of *Field and Stream*, Sheree Anderson, Stan Bogdan, Renate Bullock, Jim Carson, Arthur Davenport, Jerry Doak, Dennis Duffy, Fred Farrell, Alex Fekeshazy, Greg Gallivan, Blain Gilliss, Curt Hill, Philip Lee, Isabelle Loughead, Anne Pearson, Manley Price, Bill Reid, David Adams

Richards, David Rust, Doug Shanahan, Clayton Stanley Stewart, George Sutherland, Bill Taylor, Doug Underhill, John Washburn, Ted Williams, Keith Wright, and Joan Wulff for their contributions. I am also grateful to outfitters who supplied information regarding their lodges and their operations in general, especially Bill Boyd, George Curtis, André Goodin, Mervin Green, Hugh Hallihan, George Holmes, Alex Mills, Debbie Norton, and Max Vickers.
And I am deeply grateful to the pioneer river guides of the Miramichi. 1903 was the first year in which people wanting to guide non-residents were required to register with the province of New Brunswick, and some of those 1903 guides are the actual as well as the professional ancestors of today's guides. Their names are: Donald MacKay, Lorenzo Munn, Beniah Norrad, and Hale Reid of Boiestown; Daniel Munn of Holtville; George Brown, William Carson, and James Munn of Pleasant Ridge; Howard Holmes of Carrols Crossing; Charles Beek, Everett Gilks, James McDonald, Frank Russell, and William Russell of Doaktown; John Murphy of Ludlow; Joseph Grady, J.K. McDonald, Ben Warren, and James Warren of Blackville; Dave Manderville, Hiram Manderville, Howard Manderville, James Manderville, Jr., and Norris Manderville of Derby; Carl Bersing, George Mackay, and William Mackay of Newcastle; James Waye of Trout Brook; Alex Johnson and Edward White of Red Bank; James Brander, John Keating, and Edward Menzies of Strathadam; Edward Waye of Wayerton; Donald Fraser of Bay du Vin Mills; Louis Paul of Eel Ground; John Wanbolt of Littleton; James Connell, John Connell, and Martin Fox of Bartibogue; and John White of Silliker Office.

Guides and Guests

The Miramichi is one of the great river systems of our land; in fact, it is one of the most famous salmon rivers of the world. In fishing journals and angling brochures, it is described as the mother of all salmon rivers, two hundred miles of washed gravel, without any major rapids or artificial obstacles to impede the salmon's migration and with just the right temperatures for the incubation and development of salmon spawn. It is said that there are more salmon returning to the spawning beds of Miramichi annually than to all the rivers in Quebec put together. Every year, more people

Atlantic Salmon Museum,

flock to the Miramichi to canoe or flyfish than to any other river in Canada, one reason tourism makes the third-largest contribution to the province's economy, after only forestry and heavy industry.

Someday soon, the Miramichi River could be New Brunswick's greatest single natural resource — a renewable resource which simply requires sound management, good housekeeping, and a little policing to sustain itself. To a non-resident visiting the river to fish, a

River Guides of the Miramichi

Provincial Archives of New Brunswick

Charter members of the New Brunswick Guides Association, 1899.
Standing: Arthur A. Slipp, Fredericton; John E. Sansom, Stanley.
Seated: Ed Norrad, Boiestown; W. Harry Allen, Penniac; Adam Moore, Scotch
Lake; Henry Braithwaite, Fredericton, president; Tom Pringle, Stanley.
Reclining: Charles Crimmins, Scotch Lake; George E. Armstrong, Perth.

knowledgeable and pleasant guide can make the difference between
leaving the province wanting to return and leaving disgruntled and
conveying a negative message to everyone he or she contacts. The
guide is a part of the river, sworn by oath to protect its inhabitants
and its beauty at all times. There is no one more closely woven into
the fabric of the lands and rivers, their moods and their ecosystems,
than the river guide. To the visitor, the guide is the thesis-giver, the
river's major spokesperson.

Ah yes, the river guide.

The river guides' quality of life, their reputation, their expertise, their experience, and their longevity in the profession are often determined by their ability to compromise in a bad predicament, to think clearly and responsibly, and to show leadership. The livelihood of the guides depends a great deal on the weather, the river conditions, the nature of the fish runs in the river, the state of mind the fish are in (and if they are indeed taking flyhooks), and the good humour of the guests they work with. The true test for any guide is to spend an entire week with a guest; to catch no fish, see no fish, but have the guest leave camp thinking that he or she has had a great vacation; and to have the guest ask the outfitter for the same guide next year. That's success.

Most likely this guide would have entertained the guest through storytelling and taught him or her the ways of the river, its history, its importance to the people who inhabit its banks, and the need for the river's survival. Such a guide would have emphasized the fundamentals of fishing and river etiquette, along with the importance of catch-and-release policies, and thanking the guest when he or she released fish properly. In short, the guide would have convinced his client that there is more to fishing than just catching fish.

Guides' hours are long — sometimes from daybreak until dark, with only a short rest during the day. At high season, river guides work seven days a week. They have no union; no organization supports them or voices their concerns. Like writers, cowboys, or golf professionals, guides are, by and large, loners. They depend on their wits and their river savvy for their security and future employment. These same qualities determine whether guides receive tips when clients are successful or don't receive tips when clients leave camp disgruntled, and guides depend on tips for a significant part of their income.

The work is seasonal at best. There are times in spring when the ice stays in the river until late April, cutting two weeks from an already short season. And river flooding can send an entire fishing holiday awash. There are cancellations, always cancellations, a hazard of the trade to both outfitters and guides. Sometimes an entire river or section of river may be closed for weeks or months due to water conditions or fish stocks. All of these things are beyond the control of river guides, yet they affect their livelihood.

For those who guide in the black salmon fishery, the season commences in mid-April and runs for about a month. It is very cold at this time of the spring and it is impossible to get enough clothes on to ward off the river dampness. (It is always a few degrees colder on the river than inland.) There has never been a raincoat manufactured that will keep a person dry when facing the slanting upriver rains of April. Most of the fishing is done from motorboats and, in some places, trolling has become legal. This form of angling, though popular with some fisherman, is not generally enjoyed by the guides. It means idling an outboard motor all day, crossing the river back and forth while the guest sits in the bow with a line in the water. But, in black salmon season, the days are short, the fish are easy to catch, and they will take a fly at any time of day, so the guides' hours are usually from eight to five.

Marie Webb is a member of the Crow Nation who moved from Whitehorse, Yukon, to Upper Blackville in 1981. She is a freelance river guide on the Miramichi.

Wayne Curtis

The bright salmon season is broken into halves. The early half, which includes June and July, is more strenuous for guides. Guests seem to expect excitement in early summer. There are generally more

16

big fish, but the days are very long and sometimes hot and humid with lightning storms, and guides and guests alike have to protect themselves against swarms of biting flies. The river water gets very warm and the fish refuse to take a flyhook. In the early half of the season, guests like to go out on the river at eight o'clock in the morning, and it is not uncommon to see guides and guests still on the river at ten o'clock the same night. Most camps serve a mid-day meal to both guests and guides, and there are generally a few hours to relax before the afternoon's fishing commences. There is an old piece of wisdom regarding exposure and energy consumption: one hour on the water, even on a sunny day, is equivalent to two hours indoors.

The late half of the bright salmon season includes September and October. This is the more relaxed part of the year for river guides. Guests seem to have mellowed by this time of the season, and darkness, a welcome friend, comes somewhere between five and seven o'clock. The mornings are frosty and often breezy, but, with warm, dry clothes, a day on the river can be very pleasant. Sometimes at mid-morning, a thoughtful guide will build a fire on the ground and make tea, sweeten it with brandy, and serve it in tin mugs. The hardwood summits along the rivers are red and yellow, and the water is amber, and the salmon are speckled and orange-bellied. The water is very cold in the autumn months and the abundant fall-run hookbills seem to rise to a fly more out of anger or territorialism than the impulsiveness that prompts the hen fish of summer. In autumn, too, there is more open water available to the guide. The river residents seldom fish in the fall. They catch their fish in June and July, when the salmon are fatter and better eating; then they fish only socially, leaving the river to the guides who are trying to earn a living.

The easiest guests to work with are the ones who are completely ignorant about rivers and their fish — those who have no interest in killing anything but who have an eye for scenery, are sensitive to the river and its species and understand the guides' concerns and follow the advice they are given. Such people want only to get away on the river to heal from the thorns of city life and the business world. Big city clients are generally more appreciative of our rivers and woods than are small town or country people. They are also less expectant anglers. Clients who come from rural settings may enjoy the surroundings to a certain extent, but mostly these people come to catch fish; they don't leave Maine or Vermont and drive to the Miramichi just to view the scenery.

The hardest people to guide are the ones who have been fishing for years, who have been to a dozen outfitters before they came to this one, and who have either caught fish wherever they've gone or haven't caught enough fish wherever they've gone. Guides call them "fish hawks." They fish by the hour. These people have been to casting schools and have been taught bad habits by armchair instructors — things that are of no value, things that are, in fact, a hindrance on the river. These are people who don't see the beauty in a river or feel its moods; they won't listen to much the guide tells them because they know, they know it all. They want to call the shots, and they always measure their success on the river by the number of fish killed. To them, the resource matters only to the degree in which it contributes to their powers as fishermen and nothing more. Those are the hard ones. They are also a bad influence on the other guests in camp when it comes to observing house rules on such matters as releasing fish, hours on the water, methods, equipment, and so on.

Guide Gary Colford (front) with a happy guest on the Miramichi.

Business or sales incentive trips can also be difficult for guides. This kind of party can be chaotic, with large numbers of people milling about the river with rented equipment. None of them have ever seen a salmon or a salmon river before, and they don't really care about either. And the organizers, who may be from New York City or Los Angeles, try to make it all work by applying gentle pressure to the guides to see that key clients get fish and leave camp happy. Sometimes the signing of a major deal depends on the mood of such a client.

The river-guiding profession sounds adventurous, almost romantic. But don't be fooled. There is no job on earth more uncertain, more time-consuming, less lucrative for hours worked, and sometimes even less appreciated than that of a river guide. In fact, the guide thinks of himself as a servant. He or she is exposed to foul weather, temperamental guests, inconsistent workdays, dangerous waters, darkness, responsibility, and pressure. Yet the professional guide is expected to be at all times open, courteous, polite, patient, decisive, knowledgeable,responsible, entertaining,and good-humoured; sometimes a job consultant; and often a marriage counsellor. The guide has to be flexible and capable of spontaneously adapting to different personalities. He or she must know survival skills and be able to administer first aid. In the words of Boiestown guide Henry Stewart, "It's a harder job than cutting pulp."

David Agila holding a black

And while guides are sometimes given credit when trips measure up to brochure and magazine romanticism, they are more often left to shoulder the blame when things go sour on a river vacation. If disaster should unfold for whatever reason and the guide survives, his or her reputation is most likely tarnished for life. Guests may blame their woes and miseries, their own ineptness and intolerance on their guides. It's the easy thing to do. And the guides shoulder this as a hazard of the trade, shoulder it and keep on working.

At the fishing camp, a guide can analyze what kind of guest he has to work with simply by looking into the guest's fly box.

Most local people fish with one or two flies and no more and put their emphasis on temperature, tide, time of day, and presentation, whereas accumulating a fly collection is a tourist's hobby. Tourists take pride in showing their flies and commenting on the rivers they have fished. Sports with neat collections of classic or favourite patterns, both wet and dry, tied neatly on small single hooks, are likely warm-hearted conservationists who are content to fish shorter hours and who may not care if they ever get a fish. And when they do, they will almost always release it. These people are generally good tippers.

River guide Jason Curtis and his dog Zack work with woodcock hunters at Old River Lodge.

On the other hand, guests displaying collections of rough flyhooks, with shaggy hair wings and bulky yarn bodies tied on large double hooks, are probably looking to catch fish at all costs and as many as possible. As the saying goes, "They want to take the bottom of the river with them." They may belong to a dozen angling or conservation groups, but on the river they will kill up to and even beyond the legal limit. Guests like this may also fish around the clock, if the outfitter allows them to do so, because they want to get their money's worth. They're likely to tip below the twenty per cent standard rate. The first question guides will ask these guests is, "How many days are you fishing?" A consecutive run of such fishermen will put a guide on the disabled list and impoverish him or her both morally and financially. It is up to the outfitter in charge to establish reasonable hours for the unlucky guide who gets to work with such a guest and to make sure the guide is tipped the normal rate. Most outfitters establish these rules upon booking, and guests who don't respond favourably won't be allowed back in camp. A guide can be only as successful as the outfitter he or she is working for, and, to be successful, the outfitter needs to establish appropriate rules and stick to them.

Sometimes a guest can be unlucky in choosing a guide, too, which can lead to unpleasant experiences. These unhappy times are often caused, not by professional guides, but by what is known in the trade as a "badger." This is someone who gets a guide's badge in the spring and earns pocket money by picking up a few days' guiding here and

Gene Hill

Wayne Curtis.

there. These casual guides may teach guests bad habits and poor river etiquette, and even break laws themselves, risking their guides' pins by bending the rules to take bigger fish or more fish than bag limits allow in order to get generous tips. Badgers may carry fishing rods themselves and sometimes will hook fish and give the rod to their guests so they can land the catch. Guests often tolerate this insult because a large catch makes them look good to the other members of their parties. People like these poor guides exist in every profession, but they are a liability to everyone, including their colleagues.

At the outfitter's camp, the best guides show their guests how to fish a pool, brief them on the do's and don'ts, and then become as invisible as possible so that the guests can feel at one with the river. Yet good guides are always near enough and observant enough to know when to tell guests to wade deeper, to fish a different angle, to move a little more quickly in the rotation, or to check that they are fishing with a flyhook on the leader. When the day's river experience is done and the guests are ready to go into camp for drinks and the evening meal, guides go home themselves or gather in the guides' camps, unless they linger for a drink to toast the luck of the day.

Some years ago, on a morning in April, a sportsman left his cabin on the Miramichi. Trying to impress the other members of his party, he took a light canoe and, without the assistance of his guide, he went out onto the river to fish for Atlantic salmon. He was never seen again.

Old guides of the river surmised that his canoe was pulled under by the current because the man had stood in the anchored end of the light craft — a fatal manoeuvre in fast water. The guest had been an Olympic swimmer and had fished salmon on the Miramichi for many years. But it was the first time he had gone onto the water without his river guide.

The Guide

Just a man in the north woods,
His ways they are rough.
To live in his forest
He has to be tough.

He may not be learned
In books and such ways,
But his knowledge of nature
Is worthy of praise.

The fish in the river,
The lakes and the brooks,
Their habits and whims
He learned from no books,

But from keen observation
As he watches them play
In the ponds and the rapids
In his work every day.

As he runs the great rapids
In his sturdy canoe,
He takes pride in the work
That he has to do.

As he glides by the rocks
With a twist and a turn,
You will have admiration
For the man in the stern.

You feel safe and secure
As through the water you glide;
With a push of the pole
By the boulders you slide.

As he goes through the forest
With his packsack each day,
He sees all its creatures
At their work and their play.

He hears of their troubles,
Their worries and fear,
From the little red squirrel
To the moose and the deer.

He sees the wildflowers
Burst forth in the spring,
The ducks and the geese
Go north on swift wing,

The little cock partridge
Make love to his hen,
The sleepy black bear
Come out from its den.

He sees the beaver
Building its dam
With knowledge and skill
That has long baffled man.

He hears the great owl
As it swoops through the night,
Sees the snowshoe rabbit
Turn from brown to snow white.

He sees the mink and the otter
As they swiftly swim
When he camps by the lake
As night settles in.

He sees the wildcat
As it stalks its prey,
Sees the crafty weasel
As it slithers away.

The fox and the sable
Hide nothing from him;
He hears them draw near
As the day it grows dim.

He hears the patter of feet
As he sleeps out at night
On his bed made of boughs
Under stars shining bright.

No, he may not be brilliant
In a world harsh and grim,
But there is many a man
Who would trade places with him.

— Clayton Stanley Stewart

Roy Curtis

By the time the late Roy Curtis retired in the mid-1980s he had been a guide on the Miramichi River for over fifty years. He had worked for such outfitters as Kingsbury Brown, Richard Holwell, and Doctors Island Club. The last twenty-five years of his career he spent working for baseball superstar Ted Williams. Curtis recalled how he became acquainted with Williams.

"It was in the late 1950s, and Mr. Williams was then an active player with the Boston Red Sox. He was a guest at the Doctors Island Club where I was employed. A friendship was born, and, when Ted built a summer home on the Miramichi when he retired from active playing in 1960, I was hired as his full-time guide and property caretaker."

It was a liaison that lasted two and a half decades. It led the Blackville man into two films with Ted Williams, several appearances on Red Fisher's television show, a book by John Underwood entitled *Fishing the Big Three*, and perhaps a thousand magazine and newspaper articles in such popular publications as *Sports Illustrated* and *Outdoor Life*.

"It was an exciting twenty-five years," Roy said. "We had a lot of good times and there were lots of rewards."

Through his friendship with Williams, Roy met sport celebrities such as former boxing champions Jack Sharkey and Gene Tunney and a host of baseball greats. These meetings had been sandwiched in with hunting moose in Newfoundland and fishing on dozens of rivers throughout the Maritimes.

Roy recalled that when Ted Williams first began visiting the Miramichi River during his playing days in the late fifties and shortly after his retirement in 1960, he would ask to be driven to different rivers to fish. Because of Williams's popularity, Roy would have to hide their truck in the woods to keep curious fans from discovering the star's whereabouts. Roy had no interest in baseball himself and hadn't even followed Ted Williams's career closely. Consequently, the river guide and the two-time triple crown winner from the ballpark seldom discussed the sport.

"I was a fight fan," said Roy. "One morning Ted Williams asked me if I would like to meet former heavyweight champion Gene Tunney, who was staying at a friend's place in Boiestown. I told him 'Yes, certainly I'd like to meet Tunney. Hell, I'd *walk* to Boiestown to meet a great sports celebrity like Gene Tunney!'"

As a guide and fishing companion, Roy was kept busy carrying lunches (his wife Edna is still the cook at the Ted Williams's camp and mending equipment, keeping the vehicles and camp property maintained.

"We were together so many years, we thought like one person," he reminisced. "We had great admiration for each other."

At dawn each morning, the two men would visit one of Mr. Williams's many fishing pools along the Miramichi River, depending on the water conditions — Williams had low and high water pools. Travelling in a green pick-up truck, they would arrive at the designated pool. The two veterans took a scientific approach to fishing. They tested the water conditions against the sky and measured its temperature. They moved about the pool with an air of sophistication that is gained in this business only by experience.

At the river, Ted Williams was all business. He showed the same enthusiasm and dedication afield as he once showed in the ballpark. The two anglers would kid each other and

Ted Williams casts for salmon at the Swinging Bridge Pool on the Miramichi.

match river savvy and occasionally place small bets on the effectiveness of a flyhook pattern, the speed of a cast, or just a salmon's presence in a certain holding spot in the pool.

Roy would sit on a bench on the riverbank and watch the great left-hander work the pool. Occasionally he would shout something to Williams, a code or a strategy move unrecognizable to someone unfamiliar with the sport. Williams always threw a cast with timed precision. His casts reached distances of some ninety feet with delicate accuracy.

Occasionally, Ted Williams would be photographed by film crews or magazine photographers looking to sell a photo or a story. Roy had to learn how to deal with intruders who threatened Williams's privacy. Once a photo shot was agreed upon, however, Roy was always invited into the picture.

Roy recalled a trip he and Williams took to Newfoundland during the seventies to hunt moose. They had a stopover in Sydney, Nova Scotia, due to a ferry schedule mixup. Sydney was a baseball town. When the locals found out that Ted Williams was in town, they rolled out the red carpet. "They treated us to free dinners and drinks and literally gave us the keys of the city. Hundreds came down to meet Ted Williams and get his autograph."

All in all, Roy Curtis had a lot of good times guiding Ted Williams. "And I wouldn't trade a day of it. At what other job could I have fished every day with someone like Ted Williams on the better pools of the Miramichi River and got paid to do it?"

Guides' Talk

"Well, Clayton, how did ya maker this mornin'?"

"Nothin' again." Clayton shook his head. "Boys, I don't think there's anything in the river, if ya wanna know the truth of it."

"Not many. Just the odd lad here and there."

"There might be one here, and another in the Rapids, and maybe one in Doaktown."

"Yes, and maybe a lad up Cains or way ta hell up Dungarvon."

"Up there since June an' black as that stove."

"What kind of a lad is he — the fella you're guiding?"

"Seems nice-nuff lad, but we'll see as the week goes on. I think he's gonna be a hard man ta please."

"You could be in for a long week. He might be one of them fellas who won't be happy unless he gets a fish. Who guided him last year, I wonder?"

"I don't know."

"If the fishing stays hard, he'll get hateful as the week goes on. How long's he in for?"

"Ten days."

"That's too long . . . in hard fishing. But it's great to get the work."

"I know, ya can fake it for three days. The first day they don't expect too much. The middle day, well, ya can say we had hard luck but tell him a few stories. I use the same ones every week. On the third day, well, he's kinda thinking about goin' home."

Wayne Curtis

"I know. Eight days is too long in any kind a fishing. And another thing. Ya'll likely get the same tip for eight days as ya would for three or four."

"That's happened ta me a good many times. They have so much money for tipping and that's all yer gonna get if he stays a month."

"I don't care, as long as nobody else on the river is getting a fish."

"If everyone starts bringin' in fish it makes it uncomfortable. He won't want to be outdone by the other lads in the camp."

"Have ta get him a fish someway, by hook or by crook."

Wayne Curtis

Herbert Stevenson (left) with guide Jack Jardine.

Jack Jardine

Jack Jardine started guiding at the age of sixteen. Having been born in Barnettville in 1929, he had spent his boyhood rambling the shores and canoeing the Miramichi River. His first employer was George Coughlan, for whom he guided for one year. After that he worked for outfitters including Carl Manderville, Paul O'Hare, Glenn Sweet, Tom Boyd, and Scott Rosenberg, for whom he was head guide and camp manager.

Jack's most extended career was his nineteen consecutive years with Boyd's Fishing Lodge of Gray Rapids, where he was guide foreman, supervising as many as twenty-eight fellow guides. Among these were such river men as Arnold and Marshall Curtis; George and Norm Coughlan; Ralph and John Crawford; Charlie Dolan; Silas Jardine; Percy, Willis, Ralph and Clarence Mountain; Ambrose, Ben, Stafford and Max Vickers; Dennis and John Washburn; and Ralph Warren.

Boyd's Fishing Lodge was founded in 1945 by the late Thomas Boyd of Fredericton. The outfit's original name was Uncle Tom's Cabin. After Tom died in 1966, his son William ran the lodge for many years. In 1981, Boyd's Fishing Lodge was sold to the Pittston Corporation, which later sold to Ingersoll-Rand. These people operated the outfit under the name Camp Thomas. It is currently owned by Hugh Hallihan and an overseas group, and it is called the Mountain Channel Salmon Club.

"Tom Boyd was a fine man to work for," recalls Jack. "You always knew where you stood with him. If you did a good job, he told you so, and if you screwed up, he'd let you know in no uncertain terms. But he never held a grudge. And I liked him for that reason."

Jack has guided many famous men, such as outdoor writer and film maker Lee Wulff; Lord Belford, of England; Louis Robichaud, former Premier of New Brunswick; Victor Oland, of Oland Breweries; hockey players Dickie Moore, Doug Harvey and Maurice (Rocket) Richard, all of whom were Montreal Canadiens when they were Stanley Cup Champions in the 1950s; and a hundred senators, colonels, admirals, and dukes. Professional golfer Sam Sneed came to fish at Boyd's Fishing Lodge.

Among the best years for salmon catches that Jack Jardine could recall was 1962. In seven days in July, a small party of fishermen hooked and landed seventy-three salmon and grilse. Later, in that same July, two of the guides and four guests hooked sixty-five fish in one day at the Dean Bar in Blissfield, which was owned by Boyd's back then.

The largest black salmon caught by Jack's guests in those years was a twenty-eight-pounder. The biggest bright fish was a thirty-four-pounder caught by Ashley Colter, a lumberman and mill owner from Fredericton.

Jack recalls guiding a man who was seventy-eight years old. "It was in the spring, and it was raining and snowing. The water was quite high in the main river, so we decided to run the Renous. We put in at the Red Bridge on the Plaster Rock highway to canoe to the river's mouth. The Renous is a rough river. We had caught two salmon in the morning and were content to just paddle through. Anyway, it was just above the prison that we stopped to fish. I didn't drop the anchor, I just kept the boat's nose into the run by holding on to a long alder branch that stuck out over the water. The old fella pretended to shoot a duck that flew up the river. He lifted his arms as if he had a shotgun. This rocked the small Old Town canoe, and it flipped belly-up. With all the rain gear he had on, he seemed to float for a piece like a big garbage bag. I got him to shore, and then I had to swim out to get the canoe. It was hanging from the anchor about twenty feet out. I had to do this because we had no other way home. I swam out and got the boat, flipped it over, and brought it to shore. And you know the two salmon were still in the canoe. They had lodged up under the bow and stayed there. But we had lost everything else. It was a cold trip down the Renous after that."

1950s view of Boyd's Fishing Lodge, Gray Rapids.

Jack was known around the outfit for his quickness. He could stand with a foot on each of his canoe's gunwales, keeping it balanced, while he rode the rapids. Sometimes he did a handspring into the canoe

35

and would turn handsprings while he step-danced. One American used to bring his banjo all the way from Washington and play so Jack would dance. He also sang to the sports and was an avid storyteller.

Jack recalled that one spring there were skunks around the cabins at Boyd's. One of the sports said he would pay the guides a quart of liquor for each skunk they caught. "We brought him the same skunk five times," Jack said.

Mary Warren working on a river promotion film with outfitter Bill Boyd.

"One day we were fishing the North Renous Lake. It was very windy, and my fisherman lost his cap in the lake. I gave the man my hat to wear. He put it on and continued to fish. Sure enough, after a short while the wind caught this hat and blew it halfway across the lake, and before we could get to it, it had sunk. The man was embarrassed because he had lost his guide's hat." Said Jack, "I told him I didn't mind losing my hat so much, but I hated losing the twenty dollar bill I had stuffed up under the brim. 'Don't you worry about the twenty dollars, son,' he said 'I'll look after that for you!'"

Jack has appeared in seven fishing films, one of them done by Canadian National Railways. In this film Jack played the challenger in a fishing contest with ball-player Ted Williams. He had to greet Williams when he got off the train in Newcastle.

"This scene had to be shot several times before they got it right. Ted would get on the train with two empty suitcases. The train would back out of the station and then come in again, at which point I had to shake hands and welcome him and put the suitcases in the back of the station wagon. The people who were waiting for the train thought we were all crazy.

"There always seemed to be film crews around in those days. In the early sixties, the federal government was doing a film to promote tourism in the province. They brought the camera crews to our lodge. The producer decided that an attractive woman was needed for the film. My sister, Maude Warren, who lived just across the river, had several pretty daughters at home. Mary Warren, Maude's oldest, was chosen to do the promotion. In the film, Mary fished salmon with Bill Boyd as her guide."

Jack fished for many years with Herbert Stevenson from New York. Herbert had an ulcer. Jack remembers, "One day when we were fishing he started hemorrhaging. He lost a lot of blood and passed out several times, and he almost died before I could get help. It was a long, hard day of trying to reach doctors, who refused to meet me, and trying to give directions to the ambulance as to where we were on the river." But Jack stayed with his man until the ambulance crew who finally arrived started an intravenous and Stevenson was headed off on his way to recovery in the Fredericton hospital.

His river guide had saved Herbert Stevenson's life.

Guides' Talk

"Who's that nice woman you're guiding?"

"She's from New Hampshire. She throws a graceful cast. Ya know, women are generally better casters."

"I like the way she puts her ponytail out through the vent in the back of her baseball cap."

"Yeah, long hair, ain't it? Almost down to the water."

"Is that her husband with her?"

"That's him, he's a lot harder sport to please than she is. She keeps asking me to work more with him. He can't cast like her, either."

"Maybe a good shot of castor oil would loosen him up, no no."

"And he's fish-hungry. He asks me a thousand questions about why he's not catching anything. I told him to just keep doing what he's doing. 'They're jumping everywhere. You'll hook one after a while,' I said."

"And her?"

"Oh, she's happy. 'You don't need to catch fish for good fishing,' she said. 'Just the illusion, the expectation.'"

"Maybe if you apologize to him for the poor fishing, he'd change his tune."

"Maybe. He's a kind of expert. He likely knows that even on a good river there are days that no salmon will rise, and I'll bet he'd tell you that himself, if you apologize for the poor fishing."

"And having explained it to me that way, he'll be a bit happier if he turns out to be right."

Miramichi Gray Rapids Lodge.

Percy Mountain

Percy Mountain was born in Gray Rapids on June 27, 1925, the son of Eldon Mountain and Maude (Underhill) Mountain. He had three brothers and three sisters. Percy quit school to start working away from home at age sixteen. In May of 1947, Percy took the guide's oath of office from Al Lebans, who was head game warden in Blackville. He started guiding for Tom Boyd, who ran the outfit called Uncle Tom's Cabin, just across the field from Percy's home.

Since then, Percy has guided for Miramichi Renous Club, Black Brook Salmon Club, Bill Hollowood's Camp, Shirley Sturgeon's Bed and Breakfast, and Miramichi Gray Rapids Lodge. He also was a small-time outfitter himself for a while. "I kept a few sports, and Tom Warren was my guide. We fished mostly the Renous River and some water across from the Mountain Channel here on the main river." Percy's life on the river also includes being a federal fishery officer for seventeen years.

Percy is currently head guide at Miramichi Gray Rapids Lodge, which is operated by Oromocto's Guy Smith. Percy's wife Vearyl and Lila Kelly are cooks. Fellow guides here are Rick and Preston Curtis; Delbert Coughlan; Nelson Jardine; Dick Tucker; Larry Tracey; and Dana, Jody, and Roger Mountain.

Percy's longest stint with an outfit, however, was with Boyd's, where he guided for twelve consecutive years in the 1940s and 1950s. He can recall seeing as many as seventy salmon caught in Mountain Channel (Boyd's home pool) in a single day in the 1950s. "These fish would run up to thirty pounds. And there were a good many in the twenties. The fall runs were our big fish back then because the commercial nets came out of the river on August 30. We didn't get many fish in the early summer, except when the nets were taken up on weekends. But there was always a good run of grilse in July.

"Of course, I ran all these rivers a good many times when I was working as fish warden — Dungarvon, Renous, Cains, Little Sou'west from above Smith Forks down, Nor'west, and the main river here. And I got more rocks thrown at me than a gravel truck could haul. Rocks, bricks, spikes, anything a poacher could get his hands on. We worked up on the North Pole River, too, Bill Connors and I. We stayed in that brown fish warden's camp on the side of the road there. The Pole was Crown reserve water then. Now it's all hook-and-release. There were lots of deer up there then, too, old-fashioned deer, long-legged and tame. And lots of trout. Some wardens I worked with were Bill Scott, Raymond Munn, Dow Lyons, Ben Vickers, Ed Beak, Hubert Gilks, Eric O'Donnell, Dave Shaw, Art Matchett, and Emery Brophy.

"The river was better protected back then. I didn't like the new policy of all stakeouts. To protect salmon you must keep all the nets out of the river, and the only way this can be done is by night patrols. The last of these were in the late seventies. One night, Dave Shaw and I tried to take up a gill net down in Chelmsford. The net was in the river with a hundred feet of rope tied to it. I followed the rope into the trees and saw a pair of boots. A guy was laying in the bushes with a gun and a half-quart of wine . . . but he was asleep . . . or passed out. I cut the rope and we took his net and got out of there. He never woke.

"When I first started guiding for Boyd in the forties, the wages were five dollars a day, with an extra dollar if we took the Cains River run. There were no motorboats. In the mornings we would pole upstream four or five miles and fish down. One spring day when we were running from Shinniks Burn on Cains, it snowed seven inches on the way down. George Coughlan had the other sport, and as it snowed, an upriver east wind began to blow. We used our paddles as shovels to get the snow out of the boats, which were very slippery to stand in. My canoe was a guide's special, low on the sides, so the wind didn't bother me too much. But George had a Nor'wester, high sided, and he had a lot of trouble. I got ahead of him a piece. Before we stopped for lunch we heard motor boats coming. It was Pat Brophy and John Brophy with two sports from Wade's Camp, heading up Cains to get away from the wind. They treated George Coughlan with a little drink. At the Oxbow, I stopped and made a fire under a big, heavy spruce tree. I had the kettle boiled by the time George got there. For lunch we had fried grease. I had cooked a grilse, but I didn't do it well, but we ate it, ashes and all, after a couple of drinks. George stood with his back to the fire, and then he slipped and fell into the fire. We had left Boyd's camp at seven in the morning and we got our men back at eleven that night. That's a long day for an extra dollar.

"One of the old fellas at Boyd's always kept his guide's badge pinned on the inside of his flannel underwear for safekeeping. One day when the wardens were checking licenses they said to him, 'We'll have to see your guide's pin, sir.'

"'Yes, ya will, fer sure!' he said and started taking off his clothes on the shore. When he got down to his flannel underwear, the warden said, 'Look . . . never mind.'

"One of the guides at Boyd's was John Washburn, who is now an entertainer and a barber in Fredericton. Johnny had an old car with no windows and no heater. The sport that John was guiding had come to the Miramichi to fish salmon as a kind of therapy for stress. When he was leaving he asked John if he would drive him to Saint John to catch his flight. 'Sure, I'll drive ya down,' Washburn said, and they left. Before they got to the port city, the sport was frozen almost blue. They spent the night in the Admiral Beatty Hotel, where John played his mouth organ trying to cheer his man up. When he asked John if he had been playing long, John said, 'Yes, I learned to play on the linoleum when I was three.'

"John told the man that a chef had taught him how to cook a black salmon. 'You lay it on a pine board, sprinkle it with salt and pepper, turn the oven up to 350 degrees, put the salmon in, and leave it there for four hours. Then you take it out of the oven, throw the fish away and eat the board.'

"Ya know, a week later, we got word that that man had gone back to the States and committed suicide.

"I saw a salmon jump into the boat behind old George Curtis one time. George was very hard of hearing, and he didn't even hear the fish splash. He didn't know the fish was in the boat behind him until it kicked him. This frightened him badly.

"'And what can I do for you, lad?' he said.

"I remember guiding a syndicate writer who wrote a story about me for some big newspaper in the States. He sent me the story afterwards. He was a beautiful man. He stayed at Shirley Sturgeon's Bed and Breakfast. One morning he said he wanted to go to fish Crown Point on Renous, that's just above the Flat Landings near the old Johnson place. This was in the sixties and my old Chev was rusted out and full of holes. The Renous-Plaster Rock Highway wasn't paved back then and dust filled the car so we couldn't even see each other. When we stopped at Crown Point the sport shook off the dust. He said I had the dustiest car in the providence — he called New Brunswick "the providence." He had brought a quart of whisky, so we drank half of it to clean out the dust. Then we got a salmon and finished the quart. That sport's name was Roger Smith — what a fine fellow.

"Later that same year he phoned me from the States and said he was coming back to fish in a month or so. But when he went to get a routine medical before leaving the States, the doctor discovered Roger was full of cancer. In three weeks from that very day he was dead. Roger was a great sportsman and a great fisherman, and I still think of him.

"Another man I guided was from Brockton, Mass. We were getting five dollars a day then. This man had come for a week. He offered me a fifty-dollar tip if he got a salmon the first day, and every day after that, if he went without a salmon, he knocked ten dollars off the tip. Well sir, the water was high and dirty after a

Percy Mountain cooking breakfast for a guest on the Renous River in 1965.

big spring rain. We went four days without a fish, which had cost me forty dollars by then. On the fifth day, I took him across the river, turned the canoe and threw out the anchor. There was a lot of loose anchor rope, and when the boat was still crossways in the current, the rope fetched up, the wind caught the boat, and the sport leaned sideways at the same time. The boat flipped upside down. That sport had told us all he was a preacher, but every ten minutes he took a drink of scotch.

"Anyway, when I came up I couldn't see him for a long time. Then he surfaced below the boat. He cried, 'I can't swim!' I had to swim down and get him and help him to shore. Then I swam back out and got the boat. We went back to camp and changed into dry clothes, then we headed out on the river again. But while we had been in camp, the man prayed and drank a pint of whiskey. We anchored in the same place, and he made one cast and hooked a salmon. Now, I wanted to make sure we landed this ten-dollar fish, so I put the boat ashore over there by Al Lebans's interval. I scooped this dandy big salmon the first time it came in close. I took the hook out and the salmon slipped out of my hands and started to slide down the shore, which was wet and greasy. I ran after the fish and slipped and fell face down into the mud. The salmon kicked into the water and got away!

"'I'm gonna kill you,' he said. 'First you try to drown me, then you let my fish get away.'

"But after that, he caught plenty of salmon and everything was okay. I got the fifty-dollar tip after all. He always sent me a Christmas card and signed it, 'From your swimming partner.' But the important thing about guiding is that you have to blend with your sport. Ya gotta work as a team!"

Guides' Talk

"I guided an ol' undertaker up at Wade's years ago, the hatefullest man I ever saw. I was only about eighteen then. We were fishing black salmon. Now you'd think that almost anyone could catch a black salmon, wouldn't you?"

"Yes, ya would, Jim, if he could hold the rod and didn't have to be propped up in the boat."

Laughter.

"No goddamn way could he catch one. Everyone else in camp was catching fish. It was getting on late in the spring, and you had to cast for them, but this old fellow wouldn't cast. He just wanted to sit with his line in the water. What spoiled him was that the year before he had been to a lodge in Doaktown in April, and all he had to do was throw the fly out of the boat and he got a fish. So he expected the same thing the next year. Anyway, the rest of the sports started tormenting him about not getting a fish. We were lunching up at the balm-of-Gileads on the Cains, and they were all having a drink when he said to everyone, 'If I don't get a fish in the boat pretty soon I'm going to drown that goddamn guide of mine!' What could I do? I had to bring him back down the river that afternoon."

"What did ya do?"

"John Brophy was the head guide. I was frying bacon, and John knelt beside me and whispered, 'Just let 'im yap, say nothing.' I didn't say anything. One of the other guides said, 'We drown undertakers on this river, too.' He shut up after that.

"That was his last day in camp. Towards evening, when he still had no fish, he passed me the rod and said, 'I give up, you try.' So I started casting. We were anchored in the middle of the river down in that big bend by the old Mersereau place, and every time I made a cast I hooked a salmon, and every time I passed the rod to him he broke the fish off."

"He broke them off?"

"That's right. He didn't want a salmon at that point. He was having too much fun griping about no fish. That or he didn't want to prove me right about how to catch them in late spring."

Wayne Curtis

John Brophy

The late John Brophy was a highly rated canoeman and a guide on the Miramichi for more than fifty years. Born on the Cains, he lived in the village of Blackville for most of his life. He was a tall, rangy river man who almost always sported a mackinaw jacket and a wide-brimmed hat. He displayed all the earmarks of the typical river guide. His bronzed complexion, iron grey hair, and slightly stooped frame identified him as a man who spent the greater part of a lifetime as a woodsman and guide.

As a boy growing up on the Cains, John learned river ways as a matter of necessity. Sometimes even his daily routine depended on his canoeing expertise. John learned to canoe through turbulent waters where sometimes ice flows or extensive log jamming were very much a reality. John would often canoe to the nearby community of Howard at the mouth of Cains for schooling or Sunday Mass. One could say that John Brophy grew up in a canoe, and the river savvy he gained during his youth served as his apprenticeship for his career as a guide and a canoeman.

While still in his teens, Brophy took his first job guiding at Charlie Wade's camp, a well-known fishing lodge near the mouth of the Cains. John's ability to handle sport fishers and his gentlemanly conduct encouraged Wade to promote him to guide foreman in charge of some twenty men. Among these senior river men were George and Jim Vickers, Joe Brennan, George Hennessy, Sr., and John's uncle, Joe Brophy. Younger guides there at the time were John's brothers, Patrick, Christopher, and Joseph, as well as Tom Brennan, Stanley Furlong, Lawrence Burke, Joe Hallihan, and John and Eldon Curtis.

John Brophy worked for Wade for more than thirty years. Later he held the job of guide-caretaker for Cains River Enterprises, a salmon club on Brophy's old home stream. He also freelanced, guiding the occasional passerby who sought his services. It was not uncommon for visiting anglers to arrive in the village of Blackville looking for Brophy.

As canoemen, John and his brother Patrick won races around the province. In 1959, representing the Wade Fishing Camp and Chestnut Canoes Limited, the Brophy boys won first-place honours in a sixty-two-mile race down the Saint John River from Woodstock to Fredericton. Later that year they took second prize at a Doaktown-to-Blackville race on the Miramichi.

But the many years on the river were not without adventure for John, and sometimes disaster almost struck. John recalled waiting for a party of sports to arrive by train one evening in the late 1940s. The train came at midnight, dropping off six New York City anglers on the plank platform at the Howard station. They were to be portaged by Brophy to distant cabins on the Miramichi and Cains.

The river was in spring flow and had been rising day after day until it almost exceeded its banks. The men, oblivious to the danger, put their confidence in the guide. Here John's professional reputation was at stake, but he was more concerned for their lives. Canoeing those boisterous men through the ice flow in the dark of night was possibly the most dangerous experience that John could recall.

John guided fishermen from thirty states. He recalled a nervous youngster from Boston who appeared unable to learn the skills of fighting a salmon. Whenever the large fish he had hooked appeared

Anne Pearson of Maine watches for a salmon from the shores at Moar's Pool on the Cains River. Anne has been fly-fishing for over fifty years. She was taught the art by her father when she was a young girl and is now one of the most knowledgeable anglers.

near the surface, he yelled for John to scoop. Trying to scoop an unplayed fish without the help of the angler is not easy. One slight move could send the salmon on a run to mid-stream and possible freedom. "It's like making love," John said. "You just have to keep your cool."

A story was told at a sportsmen's banquet by a man from Washington who claimed he had fished the Cains with John Brophy as his guide. The two tented on the river bank. In the evening, while they were saying their prayers in the tent, the Washingtonian said, a goddamn porcupine walked away with John's moccasins.

John saw men suffer heart attacks after having battled fish, and one man died on the river bank, leaving his guide futilely trying to administer first aid. John saw boats capsize in mid-stream, leaving fisherman and guide clinging to half-submerged canoes in temperatures one or two degrees above freezing. He saw canoes crushed in ice jams. He saw furious anglers who couldn't catch a fish — they always blamed the guide, he said.

Still and all, when the sweet incense of the mayflower and the swamp-willow drift in from the back bogans to blend with the more familiar odour of woodsmoke rising from a fishing camp, and when, through the spruce, the winking river beckons in the sun, even the least observant riverfolk feel a pull to gravel shores and sparkling spring pools. After fifty years of river life, John Brophy was no exception. He would launch his Chestnut canoe, and, with his guest of the day seated firmly in the bow, he would paddle across the current. As he dipped the paddle deep and used it as a rudder, the canoe would remain steady. Checking the shoreline for location, Brophy would ease the anchor slowly into the water. The rope would slip through his hands and tug over a varnished gunwale, jerking tight at the rope's end to a gentle sway of the bow. For his guest, who may have been a millionaire from the United States, it would be a long awaited vacation; for Brophy, the guide, his whole life on the river was an extended holiday.

Guides' Talk

"What's goin' on tonight, George?"

"The sports are after me to call a moose. I may need ya ta give me a hand."

"You mean to hide across the river in the woods and answer?"

"That's it! But wait awhile, fifteen minutes or so after I call."

"What do you want, a cow or a bull?"

"A bull, I think."

"That's more of a grunt than a whine, isn't it?"

"That's it. Just grunt and break an old popple top."

"You got it."

"Now don't screw up. They got money bet on this."

"I won't screw up. But they'll know I'm not a moose . . . really."

"But they'd like to believe you are, so give them a good reason to."

Pat Brophy (stern) with his brother John winning the Woodstock-to-Fredericton canoe race in 1959.

Pat Brophy

Patrick Brophy is the youngest son of John W. Brophy and Cynthia (Vickers) Brophy. He was born July 16, 1928, and grew up at the family homestead on Cains River. It was hard to get from there to the schoolhouse in Howard, so Pat started to work at a very young age. He hired on as a cook's helper at Charlie Wade's Camp, just below the mouth of Cains on the Main Southwest Miramichi, when he was just thirteen years old. "The first time I ever saw Charlie Wade, he was dressed in a plaid shirt, long Palmer McLellan river boots, and riding britches. He was up Cains and he had a sport with him," Pat says.

Pat had been working in the kitchen at Wade's for only four days when he was approached by one of Wade's guests who wanted Pat to take him fishing. The man agreed to help Pat with the dishes, and when they finished they went out on the river. Later that day Patrick was sworn in as a guide by his boss — Charlie Wade also happened to be a justice of the peace. A unique friendship between employee and employer grew, and Brophy served as one of Wade's most valuable guides for twenty-eight consecutive years. He guided in the number two canoe while his older brother John, the foreman, used the number one.

Among the many guests Pat guided during those years was Mr. Howard Chivers, from Hanover, New Hampshire. Chivers owned and operated an outfit of guest camps on Keewaydin Island, which is towards the north end of Devil Island in Lake Temagami in northern Ontario. (The current director of the outfit is Sandy Chivers.) Howie Chivers was always looking for reliable guides, so he invited Brophy to go there to work for him.

In the spring of 1951, Pat and a fellow guide from the Miramichi, Bob Washburn, flew in to Lake Temagami. They would guide for Chivers for the summer. Brophy recalls, "When we were landing on that lake, which was as big as a sea, there were huge waves, and the hammering old airplane, which seemed to be held together with Scotch tape, was catching in the wind, and the spray from the rough water was splashing the windshield." He turned to Washburn and said, "Boys, we'll never see the mouth of Cains again!"

On Lake Temagami, they guided guests from all over the world. They trolled for lake trout in the extreme depths with large spoons and spinners, and in the more shallow waters they fished the small mouth bass. One of the guests got a seventeen-pound laker. Another man hooked a forty-two-pounder. A guest that Pat was guiding caught a muskie, the first one he had ever seen. "It was a long, slender green fish with a mouth like an alligator," Pat remembers.

Howie Chivers had fished the Miramichi with Pat Brophy as his guide many times. Together the two men had seen many big fish and had caught many big fish on that river. Pat recalls, "One day we were coming into the lodge at Keewaydin Island, and we noticed an excited group of men gathered at the fish scales. One man had caught a two-pound bass. They were taking pictures of each other holding the fish, which to me looked something like a big chub . . . or a shad. Howie Chivers whispered into my ear, 'Now you bite your tongue, Brophy.'"

Pat loved the river and guiding for Charlie Wade in those early years. Sometimes after the day's fishing was over and the men were lounging about the guides' camp, he would take his canoe and pole up Cains River to his home, have tea and cake with the folks, and drift down in the dark of night. Sometimes his brothers Christopher, Joseph, John, and Melvin, who also guided for Wade, would go along with him. This of course was a risky thing to do in the eighteen-foot canvas canoes they were using. The water would be spring high, and there was the Hells Gate rapids they had to go through. "Yet we seemed to do this without thinking, like it was a kind of second nature. We'd relax and drift those rapids in the dark, like they were nothing."

While canoeing Hells Gate one night, Pat saw someone on the shore giving a signal with a cigarette lighter. It was fellow guide Stanley Layton. He had capsized earlier, his canoe had gone adrift, and he had been waiting to catch the Brophy boys on their way through.

But the incident that Pat remembers most clearly happened one spring when the water was so high it was running through the page wire spans of the swinging bridge at Keenans. "I was anchored on the Layton interval. There was about four feet of water running over the flat with a lot of sand and grass in it. We had anchored in there out of the current where the water was some cleaner. I was guiding a nurse from the United States. It's a lucky thing she was with me. We heard someone whoop down river, twice. I just felt it was someone in trouble. She reeled in her line, and I started the motor and went down as

55

quickly as I could. Sure enough, just below Wade's, right in front of the old Vickers cottage, a canoe had capsized and both the guide, Douglas Campbell, and his sport were clinging desperately to its bottom. The canoe was belly up and drifting downstream, dragging the anchor. Fred Green, who was a fish warden, happened to be at Wade's at the time, and he motored out and picked up the sport. I knew that if the anchor caught, the drifting boat would be pulled under in a second. When I approached Campbell, he joked that he hadn't even gotten his watch wet. But he had been in the water a long time by then. I couldn't motor up to him because the propeller would cut him up, so I went to the upper side and came down and I got hold of him by the arm. I had to slide the paddle to the woman in the front of the boat. This was her idea. She had great boat sense. She kept our boat as steady as anything. A man would likely have been jumping around and making things worse. She tried to paddle all of us to shore. But she wasn't strong enough and we were losing ground. The water was really high and fast, and we were going farther out in the river all the time. She was fighting the current and should have started for the opposite side, which was farther away but with the flow.

"And then Joe Colford came! Was I ever glad to see him. Joe was guiding for Allen's and just happened to be going to camp with his sport. He helped us all to shore. We had drifted down the river about a mile or more from where the boat had rolled, down to Burkes Brook. As we motored back to camp, Doug Campbell was lying in the bottom of the boat. He was numb all over and blue from the cold. The nurse worked hard to revive him. Later she said that another minute or so in that water and Campbell would have been dead. But he survived it okay.

"Joe Colford drowned a few years later in these same waters. His own boat capsized when he was canoeing home in the dark after a long day's guiding.

"Some of the parties that came to Wade's in those days had as many as twenty-five men in them. One of these was the Admiral party. Another was the Belanger party, which was organised by Jack Belanger, an American who was head of the General Electric Company. These big parties wanted to lunch out on the shore almost every day. This was a lot of fishermen for us guides to cook for. We always lunched at a spot on the Cains in a grove of balm-of-Gilead trees, which is just at the top of the Long Hole. Another favourite lunching place was under the

big pine tree at the old MacDonald place, which is about two miles below Wade's camp on the south side of the main river. We had to carry our canoe seats and cushions up the hill for the men to sit on around the fire, and we *always* served them toast for some strange reason, toast and maple syrup, which Charlie Wade brought in from Fredericton.

"Jack Belanger loved the MacDonald shore so much, with its old pine tree, that he purchased it from the owner, Bill McKinnon, built himself a lodge there, and spent thou-sands of dollars building a wharf along the river bank to protect that big beautiful tree

Howie Chivers (left) of Hanover, New Hampshire, with his Miramichi guide Patrick Brophy.

from the ice flows. In a few years, though, the ice jams had taken the lodge and the wharf, but the big tree is still standing as beautiful as ever."

Pat recalls his brother Melvin bringing his sport back to camp from a day's fishing up Cains River. When he got to the mouth of Cains, he swung out into the Miramichi and discovered it was running full of ice. They were caught in the ice flow! "I can still see Mel with one foot out of the boat, half pushing, half poling among the slabs of drifting ice. But he brought the little canvas canoe and the sport in safely to Wade's shore."

Pat remembers him and his brother John canoeing Black Brook one spring during a freshet. Black Brook is a turbulent little stream with a dam and a falls not far up from where it flows into the Miramichi near Wade's Camp. "We were canoeing the rapids, and when we coasted under the bridge at the highway, the water was so near touching it we had to lie flat in the boat's bottom to pass through."

The best fishing that Patrick Brophy recalls in his many years on the river was in the spring of 1958, when he and his guest landed and released thirty-five black salmon in one day. "We got eighteen before lunch. All at the mouth of Dans Brook." The biggest fish he had seen during those years was a thirty-one-pounder caught by a Dr. Milner from the States. It measured forty-nine inches long. The fish was mounted and still hangs on the wall at Wade's lower camp.

In 1959, representing Wade's Fishing Camp and Chestnut Canoes Ltd. of Fredericton, Pat and his brother John entered the sixty-two mile race down the St. John River from Woodstock to Fredericton. The officials did not want to let John enter because of his age (he was forty-eight), but Charlie Wade told them that John Brophy was only thirty-five. So they let him go. The Brophy boys won that race. The next year they took second place in a Doaktown-to-Blackville run down the Miramichi.

Some of Pat's fellow guides at Wade's Camp in those days were George Hennessy; Leonard Hennessy; Lawrence Burke; Joe Hallihan; Stan Furlong; Joseph Brennan; Weldon Peterson; Wilson Arbeau; Jim, George, and Jack Vickers; John and Eldon Curtis; Lloyd Sturgeon; George and Ralph Campbell; Jim Colford; Malcolm McCormick; and Pat's brothers John, Melvin, Joseph, Christopher;

their cousin Clyde; and their uncle Joe Brophy. Other camp employees were cooks Francis Vickers, Jim Colford, and Dorothy McCormick, and cooks' helpers Robert Hennessy and Rita Vickers.

When the Wade family sold their camp to an angling club and retired from outfitting, Pat Brophy retired also. He lives in the village of Blackville. But he still loves the river and canoes with his sons whenever they get together. He is quick to admit how much he loves the Miramichi, with perhaps a bit stronger chemistry for the old home stream, the Cains. He has always loved to fish and canoe and still misses the guiding profession. He loved Charlie Wade and remembers him fondly. "He was the nicest man I ever knew," he says. For years, Pat owned and operated a gravel truck to supplement his guiding income. But he would always go to work on the river when the season came around and Wade's called. "There were times when I could have been trucking and making a lot more money. Yet for weeks and months at a time I would leave the truck parked in the yard so I could guide. I just loved it."

Wayne Curtis

The Guides of Charlie Wade's Camp

The fishing outfit business on the Miramichi goes back to before the turn of the century. The camps of that day were limited to a scattered few fishing huts nestled along the rivers at choice locations and were enjoyed by a precious few rich Americans. Some of those old lodges were owned by folks like the Griffins or the Pratts. The sport fishery back then meant little to the economy, and not much employment was found for the river folk in the business of guiding.

During the 1930s and 1940s, however, many large outfits sprang up along the main stem of the Miramichi River. Many of them were founded by business owners from different cities who had come to the Miramichi to fish and who saw the river's potential for the guest camp business. It was then that clubs sprang up under such names as Allen's, Brown's, Doctor's Island, Russell's, Jack Sullivan's, Wilson's, Uncle Tom's Cabin, and Charlie Wade's Camp.

Charlie Wade was a justice of the peace who lived in Penniac. In the early 1930s, he came to the Miramichi to fish with his uncle, Harry Allen, an outfitter in Howard. Charlie saw the Miramichi as an outfitter's dream, and soon after, he purchased a cabin near the mouth of the Cains. He advertised in fishing circles, attended the sporting shows in places such as New York and Boston, and began booking guests from all corners of the United States. He found a good number of American field sports anxious to visit this part of the northeast where they could canoe our wild rivers and fly-fish for the prestigious Atlantic salmon.

As the business grew, more cabins were built. These were rustic log cabins nestled in a grove of beautiful pine trees on a bluff overlooking the home pool. Each one was a lodge on its own with a separate cook camp and facilities. Each main lodge had a stone fireplace, rustic dining room, and cozy bedrooms. The guides' quarters were nearby in another cabin. Also in the outfit were an office, boathouse, woodshed, and icehouse. All were typical of this kind of operation.

In those days, each guest fishing from a canoe needed a guide of his own. Charlie Wade had hired a select group of local woodsmen, log drivers, canoemen, and farmers (all rich in river savvy) to accompany his clients on their fishing expeditions. Charlie's concern for the safety of his guests and for their success on the stream was a priority. He hired mature, river-respecting local men. Horseplay was not tolerated. All of Charlie Wade's guides were mild-mannered, humble, and generous. They knew their place in the operation. Once in camp, with the day's fishing completed, the guests were looked after by Charlie himself or his son Herb, who later took over and managed the outfit. The Wades were super personalities, and all of the guests loved them, but the guides were indeed a great asset to Wade's Camp. As well as being canoemen and guides, these

The Guides of Charlie Wade's Camp

Author's collection

Some of the guides of Charlie Wade. Posing on the grass in front of Wade's Camp are: (back row) Francis Vickers (cook), Ernest Hollier, Stanley Furlong, Lawrence Burke, Melvin Brophy and Patrick Brophy; (front row) young Joe Brophy, Peter Colford, George Hennessy, Christopher Brophy, Murdock Bergan, Jack Vickers, Jim Vickers, and (uncle) Joe Brophy.

men doubled as makeshift caddies, cooks, storytellers, repairmen, and doctors with rare remedies. Above all, they were natural gentlemen and loved the lifestyle as much as the guests did.

These men would be up at daybreak, have a hearty breakfast, and be ready to head out on the river early in the morning. In the early years, all the canoes were the eighteen-foot regular canvas type, made by either the Chestnut Canoe factory in Fredericton or the Miller Canoe factory on the Tobique River. As the outfit grew, Wade purchased larger motor boats, the twenty-two-foot canvas square-stern model with an outboard motor. These larger canoes were used for the spring fishing of black salmon.

Many guests returned year after year, and warm friendships formed

63

between guest and guide. Some of the guides developed reputations for successful trips spent guiding famous Americans. Among these guests were General James Doolittle, Admiral Thomas Gillette, Charles Goldman (from MGM), Lee Wulff, and Stillman Rockefeller.

One story has it that one of the Wade's guides accompanied a famous moose hunter through the woods several miles to North Lake. The man wanted a trophy-size moose and complained bitterly about his guide's choice of a lake. Trying to keep his guest happy, the guide walked him about the hills, got him lost, and then returned him to the same lake, the only one in the region. The guest responded, "Ah! A bigger and better lake!" Here, of course, they soon got their moose.

The guides at Wade's Camp became famous in international angling circles, their names often spoken in the banquet halls and dining rooms of the most prestigious fishing clubs in the world, such as the New York Anglers Club and the Theodore Gordon Fishers. Someone wrote:

At night up the steps to Wade's Camp they would come,
Carrying canoe seats, and tackle and salmon each one.
At the top of the hill, to the scales they would go,
Suppose they were weighing a pound heavy or so?
A pat on the back for a big fish of the day
Left them toasting in Boston, "The guides of Charlie Wade."

Jim Lorentz (left) of the NHL has fished with Wayne Curtis on the Miramichi several times.

Guiding Jim Lorentz

Jim Lorentz was a superstar in the National Hockey League for many years. He played for the St. Louis Blues, the New York Rangers, the Boston Bruins (where he was on the Stanley Cup winning team), and the Buffalo Sabres, where he ended his career as an active player. He still works in Buffalo, covering the Sabre games as a colour commentator.

In recent years, Jim has become an outdoor writer and has taken up the art of fly-fishing for steelhead and Atlantic salmon. I had the pleasure of guiding Lorentz on at least two occasions when he was a guest of André Goodin at the Miramichi Inn on the Little Southwest Miramichi.

Jim fishes with the same dedication and intensity that made him so successful as a professional hockey player. In the early mornings, when breakfast is finished at the lodge, he is dressed and ready to go. He walks to the pool with a long-legged stride that only another athlete could appreciate, a stride that has left this guide at times well behind, stumbling over shore boulders and bush. We laugh about this. Jim is not hurrying; this is his natural gait. And does he need a guide to show him where to go? No. Nor does he need me to tell him anything about fly-fishing for Atlantic salmon. While he has not been at it for a great number of years, he has been a fast learner, like so many athletes I've worked with.

Like Ted Williams, Jim Lorentz casts a long line, covering the pools of this small river, both sides and middle. He reads the water intensely and changes flyhooks with a frequency I have not often seen. And he is forever trying new things, like fishing a sinking tip casting line in the deep pools or using a steelhead presentation with a steelhead fly, such as the Woolly Bugger. Jim has taken salmon this way. Like Ted Williams, Jim has better eyesight than many anglers. In most conditions he can see fish lying on the bottom, and he watches their reactions to each presentation. Certainly, Jim Lorentz needed a minimum of supervision, if any at all.

For me, it was a fun time. When we got to the pool in the mornings, I built a fire on the ground and brewed tea. While Jim fished I sat on a rock and read. Like me, Jim has a great interest in the works of Hemingway, Fitzgerald, Faulkner, and Hardy. Whenever he took a break from the pool to have tea, we found ourselves discussing a certain passage from a novel written perhaps in Pamplona, Paris, or Key West. We compared styles. And we talked about things that we would write about when the fishing was over. Sometimes we talked about the NHL, and I would recall a certain game in which I had seen him play

Tom Fuller

Arthur Davenport (left), a long-time contributor to the New York Times, *and Wayne Curtis at Black Rapid Lodge.*

on *Hockey Night in Canada*. We talked about talent on the ice, the stars he had played with and against, boyhood heroes of mine — Jean Beliveau, the Big M, the Golden Jet, and Bobby Orr, a former teammate and now a fellow salmon angler who fishes here in New Brunswick.

Jim would reminisce about highlights from the past, like the night Red Berenson scored six goals for St. Louis in a single game, or how Jim had walked by the press box at the Montreal Forum on a Saturday night during a team warm-up and caught Danny Gallivan practising the play-by-play using a pencil for a microphone. Jim knows all the great ones and what they are doing in retirement.

Sometimes, to break up the day and to give Jim solitude on the river, I wrote, leaning against a boulder, at pools like Bluestone or The Ledges, sketching first hand accounts of insect hatches on the water, a deer coming down to drink, a spectacular sunset, or the spray from a leaping salmon making a miniature rainbow against the sun at the end of Jim's line. At such times, I put the pen and paper aside only when duty called upon me to tail the fish. Jim wouldn't have it any other way. And mostly Jim Lorentz caught fish. By the time I would get to where he was, he would already have beached and released the salmon. I have never seen Jim kill a fish. He is perhaps the most successful angler per rod hour with whom I've worked during my years as a river guide.

Guides' Talk

"What's he doing out fishing this time of day?"

"I don't know. He just wanted to go. He paid the rates, so I suppose he wants to get his money's worth."

"But fly-fishing in this fog and foam, and this early in the morning?"

"I know it's a waste of time, but what can you do?"

"He'll get nothing until about ten o'clock when the fog lifts."

"And the foam burns off. But he wants to put in some hours on the river, so anyway . . ."

"If he only knew, he could fish an hour in the late morning and an hour in the early evening and get as many fish."

"He would get more fish if he fished those two hours. Because he'd give the pool a chance to rest in between instead of wading around in it all day. He's waded out too far, too."

"They all wade out too far."

"And cast too far. Look, there's a fish jumped at the end of his rod."

"Well, I told him about the wading too deep and about the best hours to fish. 'Watch the locals,' I told him. But he won't listen. He's of another mindset altogether, brown trout or bass or God-knows-what fish."

"Well, just let him beat the water is all you can do. He'll wear out his arm after a while, and then his tackle."

"That's it. Most of the time he's fishing the wrong hours and in barren water."

"It's his holiday."

Author's collection

Jim Colford

Jim Colford was born in Howard in 1940. When he was a boy, he did not like school much. He preferred the river and woods to the one-room structure he sometimes attended on the other side of the river, where Helen Vickers taught eight grades. Jim spent his boyhood hunting squirrels, partridge, and deer. At the river from April to October, Jim fished everything from eels, chubs, and trout in the eddies near Howard to gaspereau, shad, and smelts, and the black and big bright salmon that leaped around the mouth of Black Brook as he canoed to school or church at Our Lady of Mount Carmel, the little Marian shrine at the mouth of Cains.

"It was hard to get to school over there when the ice was bad or the water was real high," Jimmy says. "I missed a lot of time." When Jim was fourteen his father died, leaving him responsible for providing a living for his mother, sisters, and brothers. "I was coming home from school when I got the word that Dad was dead, so I threw my books into the river and started to look for a job. I had to feed the family."

Wade's Fishing Camp was just a stone's throw from the Colford home, so Jimmy went and talked to Charlie and Herb Wade, who, according to Jim, "rigged me up with a boat and motor and put me to work guiding. I was too young, really, but the Wades knew I was used to the river. Back then, in the early fifties, we got six dollars a day. When Wade's had no one in camp for me to guide, they told me to take the motorboat and 'fill in the gaps,' find work wherever I could at other outfitters. Charlie even called some of these camps to find me a day's work here and there."

As a result, Jim guided at fishing camps operated by the Allens (The Popples on Cains), Alex Washburn, Stan Furlong, and George Hennessy, and at Campbell's Fishing Camp, while using Wade's equipment. Jimmy was really on loan from Wade's Camp.

"Charlie and Herby Wade were like second fathers to me back then," recalls Jim. "They took me everywhere, to all the fishing banquets and the sportsmen's shows in places like New York and Boston. They took me to a hockey game at the Boston Gardens and introduced me to Bobby Orr."

The biggest name that Jim has guided was Admiral Thomas Gillette, owner of the Gillette Razor Blade company. Later, Mr. Gillette died on the shore from a heart attack on a Sunday morning "when we were all on our way across the river to church," Jim says.

"But Stan Furlong was guiding him that day, not me. When I got there, Stan was sitting on a rock trembling and smoking. He was quite shaken up."

Jim said he once guided a man who always put on a pair of dark wrap-around sunglasses whenever he started casting. He said a one-eyed guide on the Matapedia River in Quebec had told him to do this.

As well as guiding for the past forty years, Jim has also been caretaker and pool warden for Wade's Camp. The best fishing Jim has seen during his years on the river was in the early seventies. "The river was full of fish in '72 when they took the nets out downriver," he says.

Jim has been in three fishing films. He is among the Miramichi guides who are most respected by American sports and by other guides on the river as well — the guide's guide. He is generally recognized as one of the best all-around fishermen on the Miramichi. As a consequence, his guests are rewarded with a kind of relaxation, knowing that, if they don't catch fish with Jimmy Colford, chances are, the fish aren't running and nobody else is catching anything.

Fellow guides at Wade's these days include Willie Basco, Scott Curtis, Malcolm McCormick, George Campbell, and Gary Colford.

The biggest fish Jim ever caught weighed thirty pounds. "I caught it at the Butterfield Rock out here on the main river, and we brought it up to the camp here and weighed it. It was exactly thirty pounds. We could keep a big salmon then, so there was no way anyone could lie about how much it weighed. Now, the salmon become bigger after they're released. Sports guess the fish's weight, and the guess sometimes grows out of proportion after the fish is put back. I can't be bothered doing that. If a fish is fifteen pounds, I call it fifteen pounds. You don't get any bigger tip if you exaggerate!"

Guides' Talk

"That breeze has become a wind."

"I know, it's picking up more by the minute."

"It's worse out there on the water."

"It's hard to cast, especially on this side of the river, when the wind is pushing the line against you that way."

"My sport wanted to go home. She said she couldn't get a line out and that she was afraid that she might hook herself in the ear or maybe even lose an eye. She thought that if the wind didn't go down by morning, she would go back to the States."

"So I see you taught her the old long-arm."

"Sure, I waded out and stood beside her. I showed her how to use the long-arm wind cast and reach high over the left shoulder. The hook is passing a good five feet from her head there now. I also showed her how to throw a low tight loop into the wind by giving the cast a delayed wrist action on the follow through. She's getting it out there. Hell, when we were kids we never thought of stopping a day's fishing because of a little wind."

"She seems very contented now."

"Yeah, it's a little more of a challenge, too, like hitting golf balls in the wind."

"She'll get fish, too, you watch."

"Sure she will. No, boys, I couldn't lose three days' guiding just because of a little upriver wind like that."

River guides Gordon Munn, John Curtis, and George Hubbard.

Gordon Munn

Gordon Munn was born in 1905 in a farmhouse on the Renous River, near the mouth of the Dungarvon. When he was sixteen, Gordon started guiding for Pat Whalen, a local outfitter who operated a camp on Meadow Brook on the South Branch of the Renous. All the travel there in those days was done by horse and buggy. Among the men Gordon guided that summer and fall of 1921 were the Gardner boys and Press Easley, then a famous sportsmen from Pennsylvania. "They fished salmon and hunted moose," Gordon recalls. "The lad I was guiding, Mr. Easley, shot a moose that had a fifty-eight inch antler spread. That was the last year that moose licenses were issued to non-resident hunters here in New Brunswick. At the time a single licence allowed a hunter to shoot two deer, a caribou, and a moose. But caribou were very scarce by then."

After three years with Whalen, Gordon guided for Dr. MacDonald, of Doaktown. "MacDonald had leased a bunch of water. The mouth of Dungarvon was one pool he had, another was the Robinson Bar up near Doaktown. In the 1920s, the limit was six salmon a day. We always caught our limit. But it was a different river back then. Before the headwaters were all clear cut, there was lots of water in the river all summer long. It was a big river with lots of fish in it. We couldn't wade the river in those days like we do today. We fished mostly from boats anchored out. And the water stayed cold all summer long — more shade, I suppose. Dr. MacDonald also kept a fox ranch there. Those old cabins of MacDonalds are still operating. They're called the Miramichi Salmon Club, located just on the outskirts of Doaktown."

Gordon Munn also guided for the Miramichi Renous Club, Charlie Wade's Camp, and Campbell's Fishing Camp in Upper Blackville on the main river. (Campbell also had a camp on the Cains.) Then, in the late 1940s, he started guiding for Paul O'Hare, the New York American-turned-Canadian who owned the Doctors Island Club in Blackville.

Paul O'Hare had come from 5th Avenue, New York, with his first wife and bought the island from Alfred Underhill in 1941. The original owner, however, was a Dr. Adair from New England, who gave the island its name before the turn of the century. The O'Hares hired Jim and Max Gillespie to cut logs and raft them down the river to the island, where Frank Mountain, an expert cabin builder, used them to construct the main lodges at the top of the island facing upriver. It was at Paul O'Hare's island that Gordon Munn guided for the longest period of his career. He stayed with O'Hare until the camps were sold in the 1960s and Paul moved to Montana.

At the island, Gordon developed a friendship with ball-player Ted Williams, who would drop in to Gordon's house in Blackville to sip tea in the kitchen during the evenings and call Gordon from his home in Florida every Christmas Day. This friendship still exists, although, with Gordon now retired from active guiding and being hard of hearing and Williams himself in failing health, they seldom talk anymore.

Says Gordon, "At one point during Williams's early years on the Miramichi, he had talked about buying out Charlie Wade's outfit. But it was the mouth of Black Brook he really wanted, and that precious piece of salmon water did not belong to Wade, it belonged to another American, Lou Butterfield." Butterfield had built a cabin overlooking the pool, which is said to be the best salmon hole in the world, and he had hired a pool warden to keep an eye on it. While the pool was being monitored for poachers, Butterfield, who was a dancer, held parties and dances in his cabin on week nights, free for the community.

"One day Charles DeFarrell, an artist who had originated in France but was living in the States, painted Ted Williams's portrait. It was full size (all six feet five inches), with Williams holding a salmon. Ted still has that painting at his summer home here in Miramichi."

Gordon Munn has guided many prestigious men and women, among them ball-players, movie stars, and politicians. He once fished three days with the governor of Maine. Mr. Munn claims to be the man who guided Marilyn Monroe when she fished the Miramichi.

"I fished with Marilyn Monroe for a week," he relates. "She was a good fisherman, too, caught a few grilse. But she wouldn't allow anyone to take her picture. It was all a very hush-hush thing, and only a few of us knew who she really was. But somehow the word slipped out, and a week after Marilyn had gone back, I was guiding a woman from New York, who was beautiful, too, and everyone was coming up to our canoe to see if she was Marilyn. But she wasn't as good-lookin' a woman as Marilyn Monroe was, no no no. And that was not too long before Marilyn died."

Gordon Munn has probably fished and canoed more rivers than any other guide in Canada. "I once was a warden on the upper reaches of the Miramichi," he says. "We ran that rough end of the river from Half Moon down to Boiestown many times." He has also fished the Restigouche, the Matapédia, the Moisie, the Matan, and the Petite and the Grande Cascapédia, as well as at least a dozen rivers in Labrador and Newfoundland. He has fished in most lakes in the Maritimes as well.

The best fishing Gordon can recall was in the month of August in the early 1950s. "At the home pool at Doctors Island, there was an old man keeping tally, an old man from the club. All the sports got their limit that day, and when they went to camp, the guides went out and got their limits. One hundred and seventy-three fish were caught that day, and I don't know if the old tallyman saw them all, because there were places in the pool that he couldn't see, like up behind the island. Everyone in the community who came out to fish got a few. I hooked sixteen. I think John Brophy hooked quite a few."

Some of Gordon's fellow guides in those days were Tom Harris, Peter Coughlan, Charlie Dolan, Charlie Connors, Ab Curtis, Roy Curtis, and Max Gillespie. Max Vickers was head guide and foreman at Doctors Island for many years. Other guides to work at this outfit after that were Stafford Vickers, Clarence Mountain, Alvin Harris, Paul Gillespie, and John and Winston Curtis.

The biggest fish caught by a sport with Gordon in his seventy-odd years as a river guide was a thirty-two-pound hookbill, caught by a Dr. Sullivan from Connecticut at the Devil's Back Pool on the Renous while Gordon was guiding for Wade's. "We were up there hunting woodcock and fishing. We fished out of a little tipsy canoe, one of those little wiggly lads. When we were done fishing I set the canoe adrift, before someone drowned themselves with it."

Guides' Talk

"Was that a fish that jumped just up river from your sport this morning?"

"Yes, I think it was."

"How big was it?"

"About ten pounds. The sport asked me, 'What makes them jump that way?'"

"'They jump when they're on the move,' I told him. 'Especially in the fall like this when the trees are changing colour. They come up to see where they are and to take a look at the scenery.'"

"What did he say to that?"

"'Makes sense,' he said. 'That could explain why a black salmon seldom jumps. Everything is so grey and bleak in the spring.'"

Clayton Foran

Clayton Foran is a widower who lives on the Northwest Miramichi River not far from Sunny Corner. He is the father of eight children, and he has twenty grandchildren.

Clayton was born in the 1920s in Halcomb, a small settlement a few miles away on the Little Southwest Miramichi River. He has spent most of his life, man and boy, in the woods and on the river. He is currently guiding for André Goodin at the Miramichi Inn, which is just a stone's throw from the old Foran homestead. He has been a river guide off and on for most of his life. Clayton knows the Little Southwest and the Northwest Miramichi like the backs of his hands. Consequently, he has one of the highest fish-catch averages among guides for that part of the river. At the Miramichi Inn, Clayton has a large clientele of successful anglers who ask for his assistance when they arrive.

The Miramichi Inn, founded by André Goodin in the 1980s, is a beautiful sprawling log lodge overlooking the Little Southwest Miramichi. With the adjacent cabins, the Inn sleeps twelve guests in air-conditioned comfort. This lodge has the reputation of serving the finest gourmet meals east of Montreal. Consequently, André serves many anglers, both seasoned and novice, who are famous in fishing circles. Among them are outdoor writers Jim and Sylvia Bashline, Jim Rickoff, Gene Hill of *Field and Stream*; Jim Lorentz, the NHL hockey player-turned-outdoor-writer; reel-maker Stan Bogdan; rod-builder Gary Loomis; and casting champion Curt Hill, as well as such noted American anglers as Doug and Bill Reed; Ken Foster; David Rust; John Cant; Roger Canan; and Orest, Boris, and Andrew Isztwan.

Fishing with Roger Canan at Murray's Landing, Clayton Foran said, "We raised the same salmon twenty-seven times, and each time the fish just touched the fly. In the evening, we went back to camp for a drink and to discuss the strategy of how to get the big fish to take the fly. We decided to use a large White Bomber, and the next morning after a few hundred casts and twenty-seven more rolls, Roger hooked the salmon. It weighed twenty-seven pounds and it was blind in one eye. We had been fishing on the wrong side of the pool."

On the Little Southwest, the guides take their guests to pools such as Bowers, Quam Bogan, Slatie Rapids, Forests, The Ledges, Foran's Rapids, Otter Brook, Murrays Landing, Redstone, The Budds, Pearson's, Bluestone, Chinaman's Rock, Push and Be Damned, Parks Brook, and Cleland's. These are fast-water holding pools, with spectacular whitewater riffs, ledges, and giant boulders, with a backdrop of rolling summits of ancient oak trees and stands of hemlock. This is some of the finest scenery you'll see anywhere in the whole river system. It is not uncommon to witness black bear, moose, deer, a soaring osprey, or an eagle.

Clayton Foran

Clayton's fellow guides at Miramichi Inn are Hal Donovan, Roy Stewart, Jerry Stewart, Jason Gordon, Shawn Silliker, David Hubbard, and Xavier Le Breton.

Clayton is regarded by his boss as one of the finer hunters in the province, enjoying the woodcock season and having a particular woods savvy that has earned him many trophy moose over the years. For much of his expert training he is quick to give credit to Mr. Roger Canan of New Hampshire, a long-time crony and an avid lover of the north woods.

Clayton has had a number of encounters with the black bear. "Father was a military man. My mother was an excellent cook. As a boy growing up I was a fiddler. One summer I picked blueberries and mother made three pies. In the evening she set the pies on the dining room table and covered them with a dishtowel before we went to bed. The window was open but there was a screen in it to keep the flies out. Anyway, in the middle of the night we heard the racket downstairs, glass breaking and furniture being up- set. So we sneaked down, Fa- ther ahead with the loaded gun.

The Miramichi Inn on the Little Southwest Miramichi is owned and operated by André and Susan Goodin.

And here was the bear in the dining room eating the pies. Father raised the gun to shoot. The bear picked up my old fiddle which was laying there on the chair, and he started to play 'God Save the Queen.' My fa- ther dropped the rifle and stood to attention. Meanwhile, the bear es- caped out the window. Honest ta God, I wouldn't lie to ya.

"I remember it was so hot that summer that we had to take all the shoes off the horses. They were getting distempered from the heat . And the corn on the flat started to poppin', and the water out here in the river got so low that it only run every second day. Honest ta God, I wouldn't lie to ya."

Guides' Talk

"So anyway, they went after a moose."

"Who was that?"

"Clayton and Uncle Andy."

"Okay."

"They walked to the North Lake, Clayton carrying the Snider."

"What's a Snider? I have to ask you that."

"An old-fashioned long-barrel gun with a hammer on the side like a muzzle loader. I can remember seeing the barrel laying around home. We used to play cowboy with it. Dad used it for a crowbar."

"So they went — no, go on, you tell it."

"Cripes, Clayton saw a moose!"

"Aaaah-haa!"

"But poor Uncle Andy couldn't see it. Clayton tried to show him where it was. 'Cripes! You need glasses!' he said to Andy."

"Why didn't Clayton shoot?"

"He fired at it three times. Then he discovered it wasn't a moose at all."

"What the hell was it?"

"It was a blackfly walking across his glasses."

Wayne Curtis

Eugene Harris (stern) poling the Sevogle River.

Eugene Harris

Eugene Harris was just five years old when his father died, so he had to hire out to work at a very young age. Born in Sevogle in 1916, by age ten he was working as a cook's helper at Harvey Shaddick's lumber camp up the Northwest Miramichi. By the time he was fifteen, he was working the turbulent streams of the Northwest headwaters, log-driving and guiding. He did this until his retirement in 1966. It is quite likely that through his lifetime he has driven lumber down more rivers and guided more influential people than any living Canadian.

Rivers driven by Eugene over the years include North and South

Branch Sevogle, Little Southwest Miramichi, Big Sheep House, Main Sevogle, Little River, Mullin Stream, Main Miramichi, Main Northwest, and Miramichi Trave from Bald Mountain down.

"This was treacherous work. Most of the driving was done in April and May when those rivers were piping high," he says. "They are all rough streams. We tented along the shores. We used two tents like lean-tos facing each other, with a big fire in between them. There was a man designated to keep the fires going all night. We would always be wet and cold. There was one long blanket to cover the whole crew. Sometimes the lad on the end wouldn't have much over him by morning. And we had to work rain or shine. Sometimes we'd be standing around eating in the rain and hail. The ice would be piled along the shores, too.

Author's collection

Eugene Harris (right) working the log drive on the Sevogle River, a branch of the Northwest Miramichi, in the 1940s.

"And some of those log jams would be piled twenty feet high. There would be ledges on each side. I've seen us work on one jam for three days. Sometimes dynamite had to be used to free the jam. That was risky business. We always sent two men out with the dynamite. One could help the other ashore if he happened to slip and fall in. We would light the dynamite before we placed it, so we didn't have long to get ashore before everything started to move.

"I always tried to travel on two logs. I would stand on one and stick my peavy in the other to keep balanced. And we had to pole those big boats. Joe Estey, who lived just down the road here, always built the boats for the log drives. He would cut the logs, saw them in his portable mill, dig the knees, build the boats, and deliver them to the headwaters for a hundred dollars each. I don't think there is a young man on the river today who could pole one of those boats. I remember once in April we capsized in Stoney Brook. There was four of us in the boat. We all got baptized that morning. I was wearing a heavy navy wool sweater which caught into logs and saved me. But we poled everywhere then. Hell, my folks thought nothing of poling to Newcastle for supplies and then to the old Dennis place, way up the Northwest twenty-odd miles.

"Once old Will Curtis — who was from Curtis Settlement right down here and had a game leg — and I were coming down the river on a raft. We had traps set up at the old Dennis place. We didn't get much fur either. We wanted to get down to Cruikshanks. Will was ahead of me on the raft. I slipped and fell in! With the noise of the river, Will didn't even know I wasn't on the raft behind him. He told me later that he talked to me for a long time. Finally he turned around to see why I wasn't answering him — I wasn't there! I had swam to a large boulder in the middle of the river and was setting on it. It was so windy that day that if your hat blew off all you had to do is reach up in the air and grab another one."

In 1946, Eugene Harris started working at the Big Hole Fishing Camp. This is one of the oldest and most prestigious fishing outfits in the world. It is located at the forks where the Sevogle and the Northwest Miramichi rivers join. This outfit was first owned by the Mr. William Colgate who was the founder of the Colgate toiletries company. Later it was owned by J. Leonard O'Brien, a former Miramichi mill owner and Lieutenant Governor of New Brunswick. He sold it to Mr. Edgar Queenie.

"Back then there was six of us who guided there full time — Morrisey Matchett, James Matchett, Weldon Matchett, Louis Hare, John Curtis, and myself.

"We fished all bright salmon. It was great fishing, I don't think there was better anywhere. I've seen as many as three guests with fish

Black Rapids Lodge, owned and operated by George and Jean Curtis, accommodates twelve guests and offers excellent food and lodging.

on at the same time. We did a lot of canoeing there too. We used the eighteen-foot Chestnut canoes, which were built in Fredericton. And we used gaffs instead landing nets, which is unheard of today. Of course back then we didn't have to release the fish, so a gaff was perfectly all right. They were all good years back then. I can't really single one out as being better than the other."

Some of the guests Eugene guided at the Big Hole Camp were: Allen Blakney, Premier of Alberta; Romeo LeBlanc, now Governor General of Canada; Senator Patterson, of Kenora, Ontario; Senator Aires, of Toronto; Lord Beaverbrook, who came in the early sixties and brought a Mountie and a private nurse with him; J. Leonard O'Brien; Edgar Queenie; Earl McAllister; and John Towers, who was a mine manager. These were all beautiful people. Beaverbrook and I fished four days. Romeo LeBlanc was one of the finest men I've ever worked with."

Eugene Harris and his wife Doris live in their comfortable farmhouse in Sevogle. Their family, five sons and three daughters, has long since grown up and moved on. Eugene has been retired for over thirty years, but he still loves the river and goes to it whenever he can. He owns a camp on the Sevogle "up near the lime kiln," where he goes to get away from it all and just be near the river. "I have to get away there every once in a while," he says.

"But it grieves me to see how the woods have all been destroyed. Last year I went for a drive up in the woods, and when I came home I started calling people. I was so upset I couldn't sleep that night. There is hardly a tree left. There is nowhere for our wildlife to hide anymore. That's why we see so many deer and other animals along the roads. There are no woods left for them. How do these mill people sleep at night? And the government don't seem to give a damn what happens, they cater to the big corporations. You know, we must have the worst record in the country when it comes to managing our woods. I worry about future generations.

"I don't hunt anymore. I don't kill anything now, not even a partridge."

Guides' Talk

"Boys, who was that American that bought so
many fishing pools on the Miramichi in the fifties?"
"Bob Coburn. I knew him. He was a fine man."
"Did he actually fish all those pools?"
"Only once in a while. All the locals fished his
water."
"And he didn't mind?"
"No. He seldom came. And he always gave us
permission to fish his water like it was our own
when he wasn't around."
"He was a special man that way."
"As a matter of fact, that was how I first met Coburn.
He owned the mouth of a brook near home. When I
was a kid, I was standing in the brook's mouth with a
garden rake moving the gravel into a kind of dyke so
the brook would run out into the river and maybe hold
a salmon. Anyway, I was wading around in his pool,
raking and making the water very muddy, when I
looked up and this man was watching me. I didn't
know who he was. He said, 'What are you doing out
there, son?' I told him I was rocking up the brook so
it would hold salmon. 'Do you mind if I try a cast or
two?' he asked. 'No, go ahead,' I said, 'but you're not
going to catch salmon here now in this muddy water.'
He laughed. 'Well, I drove a long way and I think I'll

take a cast or two,' he said and waded out beside me
and started to fish. Thinking it was someone from
Moncton, I kept right on raking. In a short time the
man had hooked a nice salmon on a little black bear-
hair fly with a green butt. I helped him land it. He
took the fish and went to his car. But before he went,
he told me to keep doing whatever it was I was doing.
After he was gone, another man came over the hill
looking for Mr. Coburn.

"In those early years, no one knew Mr. Coburn to
see him. A man from Moncton who had married a
woman from the Miramichi — and because of this took
up salmon fishing — discovered the Coburn generosity.
Because Coburn was seldom seen and many didn't
know what he looked like, the Monctonian started
calling himself Mr. Coburn and fishing the Coburn
water with the locals. He got away with this for quite
some time. Then the Monctonian started to run people
out of the pools. Many thought this was a strange
change of character for the ageing American. The
Monctonian got away with this, too, until one day
he approached a humble gentleman at the top of the
Vickers Pool, said he was Mr. Coburn, and told the
man that he would have to leave his water. But this
time the Monctonian was talking to Coburn himself."

Ernest J. Long

Ernest Long, or "E.J." as he is known to many, was born at Porter Cove on the Miramichi on February 8, 1933. He spent his boyhood fishing in Longs Creek with a fifty-cent bamboo pole. By the time he was twelve he was using the popular telescoping steel rods of the day.

Trout fishing in Wilson's Landing Pool with Bev Price one evening, Ernest hooked his first bright salmon. He recalls, "Bev waved for me to come down to the lower end of the pool where he was fishing. He had caught four salmon by then. He tied on a White

Wulff dry fly for me, and I cast and rolled a big salmon. Mr. Price took me by the arm and showed me how to dry the fly before I made another cast. This time I hooked the fish, and after a struggle Bev gaffed it for me. I still have the photos of that big Rocky Brook salmon."

Except for a stint in the armed forces, Ernest has spent most of his life on the river and is recognized as one of the Miramichi's most outstanding guides. He started working for Wilson's Sporting Camp in McNamee at age thirteen. One of the principal fishing outfits of the Miramichi, Wilson's was established in 1928 and now owns sixteen private pools in the McNamee area of the main Southwest Miramichi. "I had guided for my uncle, Pat Stewart, for a while in there after I got out of the army. He had built a lot of camps along here and rented them to bright salmon fishermen. But I went to work guiding for Wilson's Sporting Camp two years later and I'm still there." Ernest has guided full time for Wilson's Sporting Camp since 1972. He can boast of having guided for three generations of the Wilson family, and he is foreman and head guide for the present owner, Keith Wilson.

Certainly Ernest's expertise in angling and his colourful personality are among the many qualities that have attracted tourists to return to the Miramichi through the years. Ernest has been publicly praised as a provincial treasure, one whose contribution to the tourist industry is more valuable than the contributions of many well-paid executives. He has guided some guests for as many as eighteen consecutive years.

Ernest Long's ancestors were river people. His uncle, Allen Long, guided for Jack Russell in Porter Cove for many years. Here heavyweight boxing champion Jack Dempsey and his trainer stayed at the old Russell Fishing Camp (now Pond's Resort). "This was way back when Dempsey was an active fighter. The old pictures of Jack Dempsey standing with his trainer and my uncle still hang in that camp."

Ernest is an avid fly-fisherman whose spirits are buoyed by the very sounds of the river and the sight of a salmon pool. Through the years, he has guided American senators and congressmen. He has guided James Houston and other Americans celebrities, but not Marilyn Monroe. "I never saw Marilyn on this river, but I saw her in the hot springs of Jasper in 1953 with Robert Mitchum. That was a big deal for Jasper. I believe she stayed at the Banff Springs Hotel. She was there doing the film *The River of No Return*, and that small town was full of people trying to get a glimpse of her. That's rough country, too. Marilyn broke a leg and was in a wheelchair for a while there."

In his sixties, Ernest has excelled as a salmon fisherman, canoeman, and river guide for over fifty years. "We never used anchors very much in the old days," he relates, "and we used those little canoes, even in the high water of April and May. It was very dangerous. Sometimes I would have to get on my knees crossing that big rough river. And we had logs and ice to deal with, and no motors, not like them big board boats they use today. And we'd hold along on the pole with the bow of the canoe pointing into the run so the guest could cast along in the hot spots. I remember seeing Tom Wilson upset a canoe in a pool we call Porcupine. He nearly went for it, but we got him out okay. Tom never guided after that. I've been lucky, I guess. I've seen a lot of incidents, and often they're when a boat is overloaded or a guide is careless. You have to think safety first all the time. So far I haven't capsized. But I don't think today's young guides could do what we used to do back then. Guiding has changed a lot from the old days. Thank God. It's easier now, especially in spring with the motors and the bigger board boats."

As a guide, Ernest spends countless hours teaching fishing technique. "Most guests wade too deep and try to cast too far," he says. "Sometimes a poor guide will teach a guest bad habits, and these can be hard to break away from. There used to be a saying among guides, 'You broke him in, so you keep him.' The only way to cure a fisherman from reaching too far is take him or her to the other side of the river and show them where their fly hook is landing when they make the long cast. Trout fishermen are always hard to convert into good salmon anglers. It's an entirely different concept, and old habits are hard to break. I would rather take a beginner who never had a rod in his hand before, teach him how to cast a few feet of line nice and neat, and he will catch fish.

"The old, seasoned anglers can sometimes be the most difficult to work with. They always want to go to where they got a fish last year, even though the water conditions may be a lot different. But you have to take them there and let them fish it again. They dream about a certain place all winter, and they just have to come back to it. After they go and see it and get it out of their system, they're a bit easier to manage.

"Once I was guiding a Dr. Weinstein from the States. Well, he hooked a very big salmon at the old Stanley Lyons pool, about a fourteen-pounder. I had just got out of the hospital, and I was walking with a cane. In fact, we both were using canes. Anyway, the doctor's reel quit working. The line would come off, but it wouldn't reel back on. When the fish started to tire and come in, there was no way we could pick up the slack line. I hobbled around keeping all the line from tangling under his feet. Then we both waded out so the flow of water would straighten it and keep it from tangling. This was in the fall near spawning time. At this time the male salmon can smell the female. Several males followed the fish we had on. I scooped two or three before I got the right one."

At a recent after-dinner speech made at a sportsman's banquet in Boston, Ernest described to the guests the skills required of a good guide. "We must be able to read the water. We keep our guests moving in the rotation if there is more than one in a pool. We should know all the knots; river etiquette; the principals of playing and landing a salmon; and how to prepare a stream-side meal. And we follow up: send the guests cards after they have gone back, maybe at Christmas time." Ernest is famous for his stream-side meals and his gifted storytelling. Writer Robert Stewart described Ernest as "W.C. Fields with waders and a down-home accent."

In the spring of 1938, Ernest's grandfather drowned while crossing the wire bridge. "It was very high water and there was five of them crossing. My grandfather was the oldest, he was seventy. The other boys were from seventeen to twenty-one. The bridge was overloaded, the wind was blowing the cables back and forth. It caught the current and the cable snapped, throwing them all into the river. The water was up in the fields and very cold, nobody would survive for very long in that kind of water. One lad got ashore on his own. One fella was rescued. Two guides went

Ernest Long with guest Jean Renshaw, of Pennsylvania, who caught a twenty-eight-pound salmon.

out in a little boat, which is a very dangerous thing to do in this river at that time of the year. He was caught up in fence wire. They got him out with the cutters, and he's still living today. One young man got in close enough so he could grab the bushes along the shore, but he just couldn't hang on till they got to him. Another one was picked up in Nelsons Hollow days later. Three of the boys were from the little village at the end of the bridge. I know one guy was getting married in about two days to a girl in the house just as you come to the bridge. They buried him on the day he was supposed to be married."

Ernest is one of the few guides on the river to keep a log book. This book contains a wealth of information: once his guest, Arnold Schiffman, then ninety-three, caught a thirty-four-pound salmon at one of Wilson's pools called Big Murphy; in 1992 a guest, Richard Choan, caught a thirty-eight-pound black salmon which was forty-nine inches long. Jean Renshaw, of Pennsylvania, recently hooked and landed a twenty-eight-pound bright salmon at one of Keith Wilson's pools. One page of Ernest's log describes a fishing trip to the Wild Cat Camp on the Cains River, when his guest, a Mr. Dennis, from New Hampshire, hooked twenty-five grilse and eleven salmon in three days. The log describes the season of 1987 when, over a period of ninety-one days, his guests landed sixty-six salmon and eighty-three grilse for a total of one hundred and forty-nine fish, the largest of which weighed twenty-three pounds. In 1992, in seventy-seven river days, his guests caught one hundred and eleven fish. "Most of those fish were released," says Ernest. "These guys don't come here for the meat."

Once Ernest caught a grilse, and he was in the process of tagging it when the fish slipped out of his hand, kicked into the river, and got away. "My tag was on that fish," he laughed. "I could see it swimming around with the blue tag on its back. It swam out and lay behind a rock. Someone else may have caught it later on and saved himself a tag, I don't know.

"Once I was guiding a lady from the States. She hooked and we landed about a fourteen-pound salmon. In the excitement she kept repeating, 'How big is it? How big is it?' I told her, 'Look, there's only the two of us on this section of the river, and we can make that fish any size you want it.'"

Ernest is also a collector of flyhooks — he has over 3000 in his collection. "They come from all over the world, including Germany," he says. He has been mentioned in such magazines as *MacLeans*, *Steelhead and Atlantic Salmon*, *Trout*, *Atlantic Salmon Journal*, and *The Miramichi Headwaters*, as well as in *Atlantic Salmon Federation News Briefs* and *Tell It All*. Most recently, he was featured on the front page of the Saint John *Telegraph Journal* as one of "The River People."

In 1995, Ernest J. Long was recognized by the Atlantic Salmon Museum in Doaktown and honoured as a member of the Atlantic Salmon Hall of Fame.

Guides' Talk

"Boys, that's high water, ain't it."

"Yes sir. There'll be no fish caught until she drops a bit."

"This often happens with black salmon fishing."

"I don't want to take a sport out on that high river anyway . . . too dangerous."

"I don't blame you. But what will you do with him?"

"I'll just let him play cards with the others in the camp."

"That might work for a day or two."

"Until they get really restless."

"I remember one spring, we had a party of sports. Well sir, the water started to raise. And it raised every day for about a week. And it stayed up. It was running through the bottom step, where the steps go down over the bank. Every morning the sports would come out of the camp and go to the steps to see if the water fell. And then they'd go back inside and complain and play cards. Ten sports playing cards. They were griping about not getting out for a fish after coming so far, and they had paid big money. Well sir, it got so bad that the guides didn't know what to do."

"What did you do?"

"Well, that night after the sports were all asleep, some of us went down and hauled the steps up a foot or so. In the morning when they come out to check the water, they looked at the steps and said, 'Oh, great, the water's dropping! Let's catch some fish.' And so we all hit the river. We took them to the backwaters, like up in the mouth of brooks where it was slow and not as deep. And you know, we got fish that day.

"It was a thing we had to do."

Lloyd Waugh (front, with canoe pole) pushes off to commence a forty-mile river trip down the Miramichi. In the canoe behind Lloyd is his son, Danny Waugh, also a guide for Pond's Resort.

Lloyd Waugh

Lloyd Waugh was born in the Douglas area on the north side of Fredericton in 1923. He grew up fishing on the St. John River. Lloyd caught his first salmon in 1939 when he was sixteen years old. When he was a young man, Lloyd became a freelance guide. Later he went to work for outfitter William Jones on the Keswick River. That was in 1946. "In those days there was no trouble to get a sport six salmon a day, " he says.

Through the 1960s Lloyd guided for the Miramichi Anglers Club in Doaktown and Camp Russell (operated by Vince Swazey) in Ludlow. In 1970, he began working for Pond's Resort in Ludlow, where he is now head guide for Keith and Linda Pond. Fellow guides at Pond's are Erdie Price, Bradley Pond, Perley Ward, Rod Munn, Sonny Mullen, Ted Ross, and David Waugh, Lloyd's son.

In his years on the river, Lloyd Waugh has guided anglers from around the world. Among the most famous people he has fished with are Hollywood actor Robert Deveau; Charles Lynch, of Ottawa, a syndicated newspaper columnist, one-time war correspondent, and, until his death in 1994, a member of the *Atlantic Salmon Journal*'s advisory board; and Sir William Bentley, an English diplomat knighted in 1993 whose last posting was as Britain's ambassador to Norway. Lloyd guided an oil baron from Texas who claimed to be the first man ever to shoot an elephant with a bow and arrow.

"I can still remember Sir William standing in a narrow chute one evening, late," Lloyd says. "This was on the Miramichi. He was up past his knees in fast water. A big beaver, about a forty-pounder, swam down through the chute, under the surface, and smashed into him from behind. It really staggered him. He yelled, 'I just got hit by a big salmon!'

"'No, you didn't,' I said. 'It was a beaver.'

"Just then the beaver came up in the pool below him and slapped its tail. That beaver was really upset. I don't know how Sir William managed to stay on his feet."

Highlighting the summer's guiding for Lloyd are the canoe trips down the upper reaches of the Miramichi. Starting at Half Moon, just seven miles downstream from Juniper, where the Main Southwest Miramichi begins, parties of four canoes, four guides, and their guests make seven-day river excursions. They camp at Slate Island, where Micmacs used to gather slate to make weapons, and McKiel Brook Camp, which is located at the foot of The Narrows just across the river from where McKiel Brook flows into the main Miramichi. Another day and they are at Moose Call Lodge. It is an eighty-kilometre run from The Forks below Juniper to the village of Boiestown. Lloyd once canoed this in a sixteen-hour, one-day run.

On this run, Lloyd canoes through some of the finest scenery you'll ever see. There are ledges, boulders and sweeps, endless rolling summits of evergreen and maple, and always the roar of frightening whitewater rapids that spill in frothing turbines of splendour. This is the mighty Miramichi at its finest, deep, moody, and mystical: now babbling, now troubled with anger, rugged and unforgiving, the most spectacular river anywhere in the world. These are also the best salmon holding pools, as well as the most valuable reproductive waters for the incubation of salmon spawn, with just the right temperatures to insure a good growth of fry and fingerlings. These are demanding waters to guide in. "You have to be alert every second," Lloyd says. Patches of rough water on this stretch have names like Three Mile Rapids and Push and Be Damned.

Pond's Resort.

Pond's leases fifteen miles of river in this area and has access to a lot more. "There is a lot of very rough water in here," Lloyd said. "The river is like a saw blade. There are rooster tails four feet high in places like Big Louie and Little Louie, especially in high water. It takes a whole lot of holding back with the canoe pole. You can't paddle in this. You would break the blade off a paddle before you went a mile. You have to hold back hard to keep from striking rocks. And you have to have a good grip on the pole. If it gets caught in the rocks and becomes what we refer to as a 'sitting pole' and gets snapped out of your hands, you could be in a lot of trouble."

It was in the Burnt Hill Rapids that Lloyd once saved a fellow guide and his guest from drowning. The guide had dropped the anchor to fish while the canoe was crossways in the current. The boat pulled down, swung against a boulder and flipped over. "The sport was a man in his seventies. When I got to him he was on his feet and leaning into the heavy water which was up to his chest. But he was losing ground fast, and just below him were more dangerous currents with an undertow. I took him to shore first because of his age. Ya know, neither one of them said thank you. They were too embarrassed, I suppose.

"Many of these big boulders were such a nuisance during the days of the log drives that they were drilled and dynamited. This of course was done by hand with a blacksmith-like hammer and chisel and the old star drill, which was just the size of a stick of dynamite. Hit and turn, hit and turn is how they drilled. You can still see the drill marks. There are rocks in there like big tents. One of the pools is called Tent Pool. Another is called Blowed Rock. And there is Peter Pool and Pouff Pool. And you can still see the old log landing sites too.

"These are all great places for salmon to hold. It's all fishable water, really. In the hot part of the summer there are the cold-water feeder streams like the mouth of McKiel Brook or Ranger Brook, which always hold a lot of fish. One time Dennis Hunter drove a tote wagon, portaging to the lumber camps in there. As he was crossing the river, salmon would get caught up in the spokes of his wagon. He always got a fish crossing the river that way." Lloyd laughs.

"On the river trips the guides hold along on the canoe poles, and the sports fish wherever they like. We now use the twenty-foot fibreglass canoes made by Old Town. These weigh less than one hundred pounds. In the old days, we used all canvas boats, which were a lot heavier. Back then the boats would be shod with four shoes and a keel in the centre. We'd wear the shoes right off a canoe in the course of a summer. Sometimes those boats wouldn't even be dried out before they were back in the river again for another run."

When asked if he had ever upset a canoe, Lloyd Waugh says, "Hell, no, I never even got my feet wet.

"I also do the cooking on these river trips. It's a big job to cook for a crew of eight people. Of course, some of the preparations are done back at the main lodge. I cook the vegetables and make biscuits and tea. Sometimes on the long trips I smoke the first fish that the sports catch. They always like smoked salmon. We have a little smokehouse rigged up at the McKiel camp. I just build a fire using green alders, which makes a great smoke. This will burn very slow of course. Dry alders would be too hot and burn up too quickly."

Of his fifty-odd years on the river, Lloyd says that 1954 was his most successful in terms of numbers of fish caught. "I got fifty-six fish myself that year. I used to go out here and catch two before I went to work in the mornings." Once Lloyd caught a thirty-one-pounder. One of his guests hooked and landed a thirty-five-pounder on the Miramichi just a couple of years ago. It was forty-seven inches long.

Lloyd once guided a man who insisted on standing up in the boat to cast. "His legs weren't that good anyway. He had sprained an ankle wading just before we went fishing, and the doctor in camp had given him morphine for the pain. But he insisted his leg was okay, so he stood up as I tried to steady the canoe. He was the kind of angler that followed a cast with his whole body. So he made a big cast, and in the follow-through he went over the side into the water. He spread out like a big balloon and drifted along until I got him ashore. When we got in, the first thing he asked me was if I had any dry matches. 'You're going to have a smoke?' I asked. 'No, I'm going to burn that damned canoe!' he said."

The fish that Lloyd remembers best is the twenty-pound bright salmon that jumped into his canoe. This has happened to Lloyd on two different occasions through the years. "It can make a real mess in a boat," he says, "but the anglers get pretty excited when something like that happens."

Guides' Talk

"Lloyd, I heard you got hit by lightnin' the other day!"

"Yes, I did. It was a close call. I was standin' right here in front of the camp. I had come out of the river because of the storm and was standin' on the gravel bar with the graphite fishin' rod in my hand. Now I wasn't even holdin' the rod up, I was holdin' it down, horizontal, like."

"That must have give you a buzz."

"Holdin' that graphite was the worst thing I could have been doing."

"Graphite attracts lightning, I read that somewhere."

"Yes, it does. Everything just went numb. It took me a while to realize I was hit. The lightning went in my left hand and out my right hand. My face burned like I had gotten a severe sunburn. It upset my heart a bit, too, like it was an overcharge. My blood pressure went up sky-high. Lucky thing it happened right out here in front of the camp. Linda Pond kept bathing my face. She drove me to the doctor in Doaktown. From there they took me to the Fredericton hospital in an ambulance and I spent the night there on oxygen."

"Lloyd, you're a lucky man to be alive!"

"It was a funny feeling, to be hit in the open air that way by electricity. The only thing that saved my life was my chest waders, I'm convinced of that now. The sports got hit too. But just a little bit, I took the brunt of it."

"I heard you talking about it on the CBC the next day."

Wayne Curtis

Guide Max Gillespie with his guest, Alex Fekeshazy, a photographer and angler who owns a lodge on the Miramichi.

Max Gillespie

The late Maxwell Gillespie was a river character or an icon around the Miramichi for eighty-odd years. Born in 1908 in Blackville, he learned the art of angling at an early age but did not begin to guide until he was twenty-seven. For the next forty-eight years Max studied salmon at close range, going so far as to wear sneakers so as not to disturb the fish and donning old wigs to disguise himself. His special fishing technique, combined with his keen eye and sense of humour, made him extremely popular with such famous anglers as Charles and Vivian Kerlee, Benny Goodman, Meade Shaeffer, William Headslip, Leslie Gill, Dewey Babcock, and Everett Garrison, to name a few. Max guided the Babcocks of Connecticut for over forty years.

He was a natural entertainer with his sharp wit and outgoing personality. One of his long-time regulars, Francis McLaughlin, called him "an entrepreneur and a true son of the Miramichi."

Max guided on the Little Southwest, the Northwest, the Renous, and the Dungarvon, as well as the main Southwest Miramichi. During his years on the river, Max had more than one brush with death, and the most memorable happened one winter. "One day I was crossing the river on the ice just down from the house here in Blackville. I always used to cross right there. But the ice must have been awful bad, because I had snowshoes on, but damn it, I dropped through! The next thing I knew there was fifteen feet of water below me and nothing but blue sky above. I was lucky, though, because I had two pairs of pants on that day. The inside pair was tight and a kind of balloon formed between them and the outside pants, which were tied at the bottom. This air space brought one snowshoe up so that I could get the tail of it rammed against the edge of the ice. There were two dogs nearby, but they wouldn't come close enough so I could grab them by the tails. I would like to have gotten my hands on them in more ways than one. Anyway, I managed to make it out after a while. That's poor enough ice when you go through it on a pair of snowshoes. I never crossed there again."

Max had a reputation as one of the best anglers on the river. According to Jack Sullivan, an outfitter from Blissfield, "Max was the best slow-water fisherman I ever saw. You have to be a good caster to catch fish in slow water."

Max's biggest fish was a thirty-one-pound salmon caught on September 24, 1959, at the Doctors Island Pool at Blackville. The fish measured forty-one inches from head to tail. "That fish's picture weighed over ten pound," Max said.

Max Gillespie was a dedicated conservationist who continually gave suggestions on how the Atlantic salmon should be protected. He was also a member of the Atlantic Salmon Hall of Fame in Doaktown.

Guide's Talk

"What is the most embarrassing thing that ever happened to you while guiding?"

"Well sir, it was one fall when I couldn't get the outfitter's four-wheel drive up the hill there at the Foran Pool on the Little Southwest. My sport, Orest Isztwan, got behind the wheel and drove it up for me."

"The most embarrassing thing that ever happened to me was on a cool August morning when I was trying to scoop a big salmon for this sport . . . his name was Keith Wright from Woodstock, New Brunswick. He was staying at the Black Rapids Lodge and I was guiding there for George and Jean Curtis. Anyway, the fishing was hard and he had gone two days without landing a fish. On the last morning of his stay, he hooked a nice salmon. This was up in that run at the top of the Black Rapids. I was sitting on the bar and I ran for the scoop net. And I did something a guide should never do, and I should have known better. But Keith was playing the fish, which appeared to be holding out very deep, and I was afraid that he might lose it. So I waded out. The salmon swam around me, and in an attempt to get out of the fish's way, I stepped backwards, slipped, and fell in. Still holding the net, I had no hands to break my fall, so I went backwards head first into the water in a kind of backward swan dive. And I fell on the leader, too. Keith told me afterwards that for an instant all he could see of me was my two boots sticking up out of the water. Anyway, I scrambled around with my mouth and eyes full of water. When I came up, my first instinct was to scoop my old hat, which was drifting away. With the hat in the scoop net, I sloshed to shore, coughing and spitting. Keith was still playing the salmon very serious-like, and I was very relieved to see it was still on the hook. 'It's only a fish!' he said, laughing. 'Don't drown yourself!' Wet and nervous, I pulled myself together and scooped the fish, which was now very well played and ready for scooping. Keith Wright's fishing friend, George Sutherland, who was just above us in the pool, yelled, 'Where are our video cameras when we need them?'"

"Well sir, one spring the water was pretty high and a lot of debris was drifting down. I was anchored with my sport about twenty feet from shore just down here in front of Charlie's. This sport was a cantankerous old fellow who never fished salmon before. Anyway, the fishing was poor, the water was so dirty. He fished all morning without a pull. Suddenly he gave his rod this big yank and said, 'There's one now! I got one on!' And he started to play this fish. Well, the fish fought like hell. It would come towards us fast for a while and then suddenly it would start going the other way, and there was nothing he could do but let it go. Twice it took almost all his line. I said, 'It must be a very big fish. We'll have to go ashore.' 'God, I'd give anything to land this one,' he said. So, carefully I pulled the anchor and paddled the boat to shore backwards, giving him lots of freedom to work with his fish. Ashore, he got out and backed up on the bank and reeled away, picking up some of the line as I got the scoop net ready. But I thought it was kind of funny that this fish never once jumped or attempted to break water. Anyway, we were standing there trying to get a glimpse of the fish when I saw it coming! My heart sank."

"What was it?"

"He was hooked into a piece of alder about four feet long, which had a kink in it, and the hook was just to one side of the crooked part. And that's what was giving him the fight. When it got crossways in the strong water, he couldn't hold it. And then it would swing and come his way fast, and he wouldn't be able to reel in quick enough to pick up the line. He thought he had hooked an extra-great fighter, and so did I. He was really disappointed when he saw the piece of alder branch twisting and turning in the current as it come toward us."

"It's always better if something like that happens to someone else."

Guy Silliker

Born on the Little Southwest Miramichi in 1918, Guy Silliker grew up loving the river so much that he quit school during his teens and went to work as a log driver and river guide. He drove logs on the Little Southwest, the Northwest Miramichi, and the North Pole Stream. Later he became famous for his canoemanship, running the turbulent waterways with clients from all over the world in search of high adventure. Guy has built more than twenty canvas canoes (without using moulds) as well as plywood motorboats, used for black salmon. He has also been a community fly-tyer, making more than 2800 flyhooks each year. Indeed, throughout his sixty-odd years as a guide, Guy has built a reputation as one of the most colourful and knowledgeble river men in New Brunswick.

He was really an expert canoeman, and this was what his clients wanted from him — to canoe and fish the wild upper reaches of these rivers. "There were canoe trips three or four days at a time," Silliker says. "We'd be tenting along the shores and repairing the boat every now and then. The water was very fast and there were boulders as high as your head to canoe around. In places like Little Falls and Ramsey Rock, it was hard. Sometimes we'd have to portage the canoe over ledges."

Guy did not employ himself with any particular outfit but rather worked as a freelance guide. He recalls that one of his first clients was a man by the name of Guy Johnston, who came from the United States in 1935 looking for his first black salmon. "We canoed the little Southwest that spring and got more fish than I'd care to mention. Johnston died in the fall of 1936."

Guy guided Mr. Cossaboom, who invented the Cossaboom flyhook in a cabin on the upper reaches of the Little Southwest, where they were fishing. Another man who invented a flyhook while being guided by Guy was Scott Fraser, of Montreal, who later built a camp on the river and hired Guy as a caretaker. He called his fly the Irritator. Guy also guided Mr. Fred Adams, whose company made Chiclets. This famous chewing gum, of course, was not invented while Adams was fishing on the Miramichi with Guy Silliker.

Guy recalls that his most successful day's fishing was in the 1970s, when his group got twenty-one salmon before noon. "I could almost say it was before breakfast, but I did have a cup of instant coffee and a slice of toast." His biggest fish caught to date is a twenty-eight-pound fall salmon, "caught out here in front of the house years ago. But a sport I was guiding, an Italian lad, caught a thirty-two-pound black salmon one spring up near the Somers Bridge."

Guy is one of the few New Brunswick guides to have been guided himself by the great Richard Adams on his home stream, the Matapédia, when Silliker was *his* guest. Another of Guy's river cronies

Guy Silliker

is Gary Anderson, a McGill University professor who owns a cabin on the Miramichi and who has written several books on Atlantic salmon and salmon fishing. In his books, Anderson often recalls his experiences with Guy, who has also been written about in magazines such as *Field and Stream, Outdoor Life, Atlantic Salmon Journal,* and *Eastern Woods and Waters.*

Guides' Talk

"Where did you guide last year?"

"I worked as a travel guide for Z-Tours, a company out of Interlaken, Switzerland."

"That sounds interesting. You worked with Europeans then?"

"Yes, from May to the end of October, I canoed the Cains at least twenty-five times. We put in at Salmon Brook and ran down to the river's mouth and on down the main river to our hauling-out place at the old Fisher camp. It was a nice one-day excursion. The Europeans loved the river, and we often saw deer and moose and other wildlife. We always lunched at the Ledges above where the hydro lines cross the river, and took photos. They wanted pictures of each other in the wilds of Canada. Sometimes during this mid-day meal, guests would recline on the shore for a while, maybe even have a drink of cool beer before we pushed on. Sometimes during those hot days of summer, the guests wanted to stop at the Long Hole and swim, then we would suntan afterwards, laying in the canoes and letting the sun dry us. My only responsibility as guide was to make sure that everyone had a good day and got home safely.

"One day in mid-October, I was guiding a group of five canoes. A doctor, who was a very big man, and his wife were in the rear canoe when they capsized in that little run at the foot of Brophy's Island. Their light canoe had gotten crossways in the run, caught an exposed rock and flipped over. I was leading the fleet and happened to turn to see the canoe coming bottom-up with the doctor and his wife under it. Perhaps I should have been at the rear. In any case, I paddled back to assist them to shore, picking up their drifting paddles and cushions as I went. The water was not deep so there was no danger of them drowning, but it was a very cold day with an upriver wind. The couple sloshed to shore and stood shivering as I dragged their half-submerged boat onto the rocks and emptied the water from it. Just around the bend was a cabin that was owned by the Wades. Under the circumstances, I would have been justified in breaking into it, building a fire, and calling for someone to come after us. I suggested this. But the Germans would have no part of it. 'We go on by boat,' they said. Then I suggested that maybe it would be a good idea if we put one of them in with an experienced canoeist. But they would have no part of that, either. 'We start the journey together, and we end it together,' they said. So they paddled through the afternoon, facing that cold upriver wind, pale as two corpses. One of the other Germans treated them with scotch whisky along the way. When we reached the Fisher camp, they had developed hypothermia and had to be helped up the hill to where they could undress beside a warm oil heater and take hot showers and have hot drinks. The next day, they gave me gifts and laughed about the incident when I asked if they had been in for a swim lately. But at the time it was not very funny at all."

Dale Norton

Debbie Norton

Debbie Norton is the daughter of Harry and Rita (Holmes) Blackmore, who owned and operated Blackmore's Fishing Camp on the Little Southwest Miramichi. She was born in Sillikers on January 2, 1956. The Blackmore family has long been associated with the outfitting and guiding industry. Harry looked after leases at the Forks of the Little Southwest and the North Branch of the Little Southwest for Grover Lassen from 1957 to 1965. Harry guided and Rita cooked for the guests. It was in this area that Debbie, at age two, got lost in the woods when she followed her father, who had gone up the river to fish. She was later found by her mother on a fishing trail. Debbie had sauntered down to watch the boats come in, fascinated with the whole experience of salmon angling even then. When she was three, little Debbie fell into the river and almost drowned before her brother Fred, who was poling a canoe nearby, rescued her.

When Debbie was seven years old, she spent the summer fishing with her father. They landed twenty-one salmon and a barrel of grilse in their home pool on the Little Southwest. Harry would hook the fish and give the rod to Debbie to bring them in. And it never mattered to Harry if Debbie lost a salmon. "It seemed he could hook a fish whenever he wanted to," Debbie says now. She recalls that, in the sixties, "salmon were so plentiful they were running between our legs when we were wading." Debbie hooked and landed her first salmon while fishing at the Oxbow when she was ten years old. By that time she was able to pole a canoe as well as any guide on the river.

When Debbie was eighteen she acquired a guide's licence and has been guiding part-time ever since. Debbie has a master's degree in career guidance and is a counsellor at North and South Esk Regional High School in Sunny Corner. But it is the river guiding she loves most, and this she does seasonally, working out of the old home outfit, now called The Upper Oxbow Outdoor Adventures, which she and her husband Dale own. The business still uses the old Blackmore fishing camps that have been in the family since 1935.

A guest whom Debbie was guiding last year hooked a clam on a Golden Eagle, which is a spring streamer. The water was dirty and she had asked him to fish deep. Debbie's biggest catch to date is a fifteen-pounder caught five years ago in the home pool. In 1995, Debbie caught and released eighteen grilse and three salmon.

Debbie is a board member of the Northumberland Salmon Protection Association, a conservation group. She also sits on the policy and regulations committee, which is part of the Miramichi Watershed Committee.

Debbie Norton

Debbie loves the river; she loves giving advice on how to cast a flyhook, which fly to use, and where the best salmon lies are, and she also loves preparing good stream-side meals and main course dinners in the lodge. She is one of the most respected guides on the river, and many of her guests ask for her to guide them personally. She says she picked up her river traits from her father and her cooking expertise from her mother. Debbie Norton might well be the only river guide on the Miramichi who can please guests to this degree, ensuring that they are looked after both on the river and at the dinner table.

Guides' Talk

"How's she goin' now, Jason?"
Jason shakes his head.
"Nothin', eh?"
Jason shakes his head again.
"Been here long?"
"Couple hours."
"What's he using?"
"A big bear-hair double."
"He might jig one."
"He hooked onto that big rock down in that hole
there awhile ago. He thought for sure he had a fish on.
The fast water almost pulled the rod out of his hand.
'There, I struck one,' he said, and he give the rod a yank.
"'There's always a big one in that hole,' I told him.
'Just throw 'er back in there and brace your feet.' He's
happy now. Back at the camp tonight, he'll have
hooked a fish. Maybe even had 'im on for a jump or
two. A couple of scotch will make 'em jump."
"We've got some good stories out of that rock this
summer."

Sherman Hines

122

Charlie Connors, a guest, Ralph Warren, and Dorothy Routh.

Ralph Warren

Ralph Warren and his wife Edna live in Gray Rapids. Ralph was born in this part of the Miramichi in 1921. Except for his years overseas serving his country in World War II, Ralph has spent most of his lifetime in the woods and at the river. He is known in Miramichi as an excellent hunter, and for many years he was an active trapper. Ralph probably knows more about the province's interior, its lakes, rivers and woods, than any other river guide on the Miramichi.

Ralph says he once had a pet beaver that was a great help to him in learning the ways of the woods. "The beaver travelled with me for years, building old camps and gathering firewood. One fall we moved into an abandoned log cabin on the Dungarvon, the beaver and I. The cabin had been left empty for years and was full of cracks, the chinking having fallen away from between the logs. I worked all afternoon gathering moss, intending to caulk the camp the next morning. I had a huge pile of moss on the cabin floor. Anyway, I went to bed and ya know that beaver worked all night. When I got up in the morning he had the camp caulked up as high as he could reach. And that's the truth!"

One summer Ralph and Arch Jardine were staying at a similar log cabin on the Cains River. "We were up there fishing trout," he says. "The flies were so thick that one morning I woke up and found that, during the night, the mosquitoes had dragged me out into the yard — I was smaller than Arch, ya see."

Ralph started guiding in 1950. His first job was with Kingsbury Brown, who operated a big outfit of fishing camps (now owned by Black Brook Salmon Club) at Six Mile Brook on Cains River. During the sixties, after this stint with Brown, he started guiding for Paul O'Hare, who for years owned and operated the Doctors Island Club at Blackville. He stayed with Paul for nearly ten years. But Ralph's longest employment as a river guide was with Boyd's Fishing Lodge in the Rapids, where he worked for Fredericton's Bill Boyd for more than fifteen years. "My foreman at Boyd's during those years was Jack Jardine," Ralph recalls. "Jack was a good man to work for, as was Bill Boyd. We had one of the truly great salmon pools on the main river — the Mountain Channel — so I enjoyed my years there. We always caught fish, regardless of conditions." Ralph also guided for Wade's Fishing Lodge, Miramichi Renous Club, Curtis Fishing Camp, and Jack

The upper Miramichi River.

Clayton Stanley Stewart

Routh, an American who bought the Dean Bar Lodge and Pool from Boyd. Ralph is still a frequent stopper-by at Dean Bar Lodge and a valuable friend to Jack and Dorothy Routh.

Ralph recalls guiding a dentist from Lyndhurst, New Jersey, during the sixties when he was working for Paul O'Hare. "Dr. Losier was a good fisherman and one of Paul's regulars. I guided him for years. One day we were at the Gray Rapids pool, one of Losier's favourites. It was a raw, miserable fall day, and it was raining, so Dr. Losier decided after an hour or so that he would quit fishing and go back to camp. We were very cold when we got to the car, which was in the parking lot at the top of the hill. There, Dr. Losier opened a bottle of good scotch, and we had a drink, which warmed us up a bit. Halfway back to camp he stopped the car and we had another big drink, which heated us up quite a lot more. By the time we got to camp, we had drunk more scotch, and the weather had moderated considerably."

Ralph said that the best salmon fishing he has ever seen during his years on the river was in 1972. "You could get a fish almost any place at all that year. Just wherever you happened to go over the hill to the river, you threw a line in and hooked one. My lawn didn't get mowed all that summer, there just wasn't time."

Guides' Talk

"Pat, that's a cold ol' upriver wind, ain't it?"

"Boys, it is so. It seems to blow right through a person this time of the year."

"I know. Like it would clothes on a line."

"When that wind is blowing, the river seems to haunt me some way, especially in the fall like this."

"I know. I just finished guiding a beautiful woman from the States. She owns a horse farm down there. She was here for over a week, and we had some great conversation. Boy, I hated to see her go!"

"I saw you with her. She was a good looking woman . . . and a good caster."

"She was a beautiful person all around. I'm glad you could see her personality in the cast."

"The wind is always more penetrating when you're left alone after being with company like that. And it's never a good time to say goodbye, she wrote that to me in a little note she left with my tip money back at the lodge."

"I think a river is the loneliest place there is sometimes."

"I know. After she was gone my insides felt like ashes."

"But that's all in the mind, not the place. And another part of the job we have to deal with."

"I guided two old men from Maine for a few days after that, nice men, too. But I still had the horse farm on my mind, and I don't think I did a very good job. I just couldn't get into it."

Bob Miller

John Curtis

John D. Curtis has guided on the Miramichi for forty years. It's hard for me to tell his story objectively, because he is my father.

One of the first experiences I can remember sharing with my father is his taking my brother Winston and me to Newcastle, where he bought us each a fishing rod at Stothart's Mercantile store. I was no more than six. The next day our family went to Morse Brook, which flows through the woods a mile or so behind our home. At a beaver dam, we got a few trout, which I strung on an alder branch to carry home proudly. We had a picnic on the shore. Mother was a pretty woman in her thirties then. She would wear my father's flannel shirts over her slacks, and a pair of his work boots, and she would make the picnic lunch and come with us to the brook. Sometimes we still do this on the twenty-fourth of May as a kind of family tradition. When I think of my mother back then, I feel she may have been slightly ahead of her time when it came to fashion. Of course, she didn't wish to be seen in these clothes, and that outfit was only for the eyes of her own young family. It was a sharp contrast to the 1940s spike heels and pleated skirts I remember her wearing at home and to church on Sundays. We fished the brook a lot when we were little, and after a couple of years we were allowed to go to the river to fish for our first salmon.

When I look through old family albums, I see many photos of father standing with two or three sports (whose names are long since forgotten), with a dozen salmon spread on the grass before them. Perhaps these were from a day's fishing at home here on the Miramichi, or maybe they are catches from three-day runs down the Cains, which were common after Father started outfitting in the 1950s. Also in those old albums I see my brothers and sister and me as children, standing with our first salmon, paddling canoes with our spindly arms, or perhaps posing on the roof of some fishing camp still under construction.

The river and fishing have always been a part of our family. John Curtis was born in the community of Howard on the Miramichi on September 15, 1911, the son of Thomas and Barbara (Sullivan) Curtis. He and mother, Brycie (Coughlan), live on the homestead which Daddy inherited from his father, who inherited it from his Aunt Sarah Nutbeam. Father and Mother raised a family of four sons and a daughter, all river rats. My sister Daphne caught her first big salmon when she was eight years old and was a decent guide when she was in her mid-teens. For sixty-odd years, father worked as a woodsman, farmer, storekeeper, guide, and outfitter. He divided his time among these occupations, and I believe he had the most satisfying career that anyone could ever wish for. "The river keeps us all sane," he would say. "Whenever we get up tight from stress or hard work, we go to the river."

When we were children, we were never allowed to fish on Sundays. Instead, we dressed in our best clothes and attended the services of Reverend Jim Morgan at Trinity Anglican Church in Blackville, where we filled an entire pew. When Mr. Morgan built a bigger church in the 1960s, Father donated logs from his woodlot. Years later, that church, where our aunt Sarah Nutbeam and her family are buried, was declared a historic site after my brother Herbie and others campaigned to save it from demolition. Sometimes, after we came home from church, my brother Winston would disappear. I would go to the river and find him lying in

Buttermilk Brook Pool on Cains River.

the boat in his Sunday clothes, his eyes hooded with his palms, staring, mesmerized, into the water. As we got a little older, we started fishing on Sundays anyway. At first we would steal away to the river where our rods were hidden. Later we went more openly, until eventually Father decided that maybe Sunday fishing wasn't a sin, that the river was a gracious thing, and that he could fish with us without a guilty conscience — but only after church. Father sold tobacco in his store, but as children we were never allowed to smoke around home. We smoked at the river. Father never smoked or drank, and while some of us in the family now have these habits and practice them openly, I know he still believes them to be cardinal sins.

When Father was a small boy, he was sitting on the end of Grandfather's canoe one spring evening, fishing with an angleworm. The boat was moored at the Cavanaugh Eddy not far from home. Suddenly, a large moose came out of the woods at full gallop. Chased by dogs, it crashed over the river bank and into the boat, breaking it into splinters and knocking Father into the river. He clung on to the boards and used the bushes to drag himself back to shore. "To this day, when I go to the eddy, I think of that moose," he says.

To fifth-generation inhabitants like ourselves, the river is a place to work and a place to play — a family resource which still supplies those of us who are more enthusastic with seasonal guiding and maybe a fish for the table. But mostly it has become a year-round recreational area with fly-fishing, canoeing, and skating in winter. And I can still see and smell the great bonfires of my boyhood, a distant blaze on a river forever frozen in time.

The river has also haunted the family metaphorically. When we gather at home on holidays, we congregate in one of the family fishing camps, telling yarns and reweaving tapestries of our history spun from the heavy silk-threaded bamboo rods of my father's early years to the modern lightweight graphite and boron rods we now use. The grandsons and granddaughters of the family join in these festive hours, which always include a potluck dinner. In smaller groups, the younger ones relive experiences, lesser perhaps, and still unbrushed by the magic of time. On Christmas nights, when we jam around Mother's piano, there are fly boxes, vests, lines, and waders under the tree, and it has been that way for as long as I can remember.

On Thanksgiving Day, we gather in Father's old cabin, the ancient guns still hanging on the walls. When he was a young man Father was a deer hunter. He has probably shot as many trophy deer per hours spent hunting as any man in the county. He always hunted with a 43-caliber German Mauser, which he purchased from Charlie Campbell for three dollars and which, he claimed, was so long in the barrel that he had to stand it on end to swing it in heavy woods.

Sometimes other hunters criticized him for using the ancient black-powdered gun. "That's my lucky old gun," he would say. "It never lets me down."

In the 1950s, on fall evenings, father would go for his "walk" with the gun (he never called it hunting). Gary and I would hang around in our dooryard and listen for the boom of the Mauser. We recognized the sound of every gun in our small community and listened for them until well after dark. Sometimes we'd hear Francis Vickers's 38-55 Winchester, sometimes Clark Keenan's 300 Savage, sometimes Arnold Campbell's 30-30 Marlon, sometimes the Mauser. And we would wait eagerly for father to come out of the darkened woods to relive the experience, first to Mother. Father always hated to kill and could never butcher a farm animal. Still, hunting for survival had been in his blood for generations, and this, I now believe, became a torture to him long before any of us children knew or understood it.

Father joked that he strained the Mauser once by firing at a deer which was out of range. One October evening in 1957, he was shooting at a deer when the old gun held fire. When he opened the chamber to reload, it discharged, wounding him in the arm. He was laid up in hospital for a long time. His personal superstitions led him to think that maybe this was an omen, so he retired the gun and pretty much gave up hunting.

Early on, as a river guide, father was employed with Alex Washburn, Boyd's Fishing Lodge, Doctors Island Club, and Charlie Wade's Camp. In the fifties he built cabins and started his own small outfitting business. In his words, "On this part of the Miramichi, the fishing was so good that we had to hide behind trees to tie our hooks on the line."

Many sport fishers came from Maine, New Hampshire, Connecticut, and New York to our place year after year. They came in the spring to fish the black salmon, returning in summer for bright fish, and again in the fall for the canoe runs down the lower reaches of the Cains for both woodcock and salmon. Among these guests were Tom Ritchie, Al Beternick, Al Hanson, Art Flick, Louie Eagles, Henry Galler, Evans Page, and Dr. Niles Perkins, a heart surgeon from Bowdoinham, Maine, who drowned in the spring of 1972 when he went out on the river without his guide. "Niles dropped the anchor while he was standing in the anchor end, and the boat fish-tailed," Father said. "He was a good swimmer, but the water was high and just one degree above freezing. No one could survive in it for more than a few minutes."

It was here that David Egan, from Guildford, Connecticut, first got interested in Atlantic salmon angling and salmon conservation. In 1975, he founded the Connecticut River Salmon Association, a conservation group with the goal of restoring Atlantic salmon runs to the once-great Connecticut River watershed.

Father told us that Grandfather once found a dead salmon and a dead eagle clamped together on the shores of Cains River up near the mouth of the Sabbies. Apparently, the eagle had grabbed the big salmon and tried to lift it from the water. Its talons were clamped into the fish. But the salmon was too big to lift, and it had towed the eagle into the deep water. Both the fish and the bird had died, clasped together. "There is a great lesson in this. We should never get too greedy in life," Father said. "Even on the river we tend to expect too much. A small fish can be as much fun as a big one, or even no fish at all can be fun if everything else is right with the world."

It seems that my family has always been intrigued in some way by the river. Great-great-grandfather John Curtis swam across it at the Strawberry Marsh in Newcastle in 1818 to marry Ann Applin, who had just arrived in Nelson by ship. It was said that he forgot the ring and had to swim the river twice. Great-grandfather David sought the job of channel-finder for the river boat *Andover* on its Doaktown run, and my grandfather — Papa — fished with a spear to supply his large family with fish for the table. He was a log driver and a stuntman who practiced his hand springs out on logs that drifted past. I can remember him telling us children of Joe Smith, a poet and a song writer, who helped him spear a wagon-load of fish at the Salmon Hole on Dungarvon to supply a lumber camp for the winter. They burned pitch-wood in a wire crew pot which lit up the water, attracting salmon to within reach of the spear. Maybe these are some reasons why our attraction to the river is second nature.

Father worked the river, too — the log drives in Morse Brook, Black Brook and up on the Cains, as well as the great corporation drives down the Miramichi at the end of May, which ended during the early sixties. Father experienced all of this to a lesser degree than Grandfather did. In his own time, Father saw the river transform from a means of transportation and a food supply to a no-less-important river of recreation, outfitting, angling, and guiding.

Father, who is mild-mannered, recalled guiding a disgruntled American back in the early seventies when the river was full of fish. "Salmon were jumping all around us," but the man, not being very successful, complained bitterly about the river. "He did not see the scenery, hear the birds, or smell the blossoms on that June morning. He kept griping because he couldn't hook a fish. I was ready to hit him with the paddle. The guide who had him before me had put him out on the shore and made him walk back to camp. So I asked him, 'Sir, did you come here to fish or to fight?'" While father was paddling him back to camp after three hours of futile casting, a ten-pound salmon jumped into the canoe almost on the fisherman's lap. "He put his big sneakers down on the salmon! He couldn't much blame the river after that."

Father was a crony of the late Wallace Doak, the famous fly-tyer from Doaktown. As young men during the thirties, they had worked in the woods together around Doaktown. They each decided to open a retail business. In 1946, Wallace opened a fly-tying shop in front of his home on main street in Doaktown, and my father built a grocery store on the old home property on the Howard Road. This kind of country store is a grandparent to the convenience stores we know today. Through the 1950s our store was a kind of community meeting place. The men, who were woodsmen, truckers, farmers, and guides, came and sat out the long storms of winter. Their tobacco smells mixed with those from the woodstove, the barrels of corned beef and molasses, and the bulks of candy. There was always storytelling, and tales tall and true filled the nights. Other evenings there might be a card game. Sometimes a Jimmie Rodgers railroad song was rendered by the proprietor. Often, late into the night, the wives of the community came to collect their husbands. Occasionally Doaktown's Dr. John Hamilton, wearily awaiting the arrival of a new baby in the community, stopped to kill time, and sometimes the Doaktown Mounties dropped by.

In summer, the guides congregated on the back steps of father's warehouse to spend the evening playing music and planning strategies for the following day's work. And they always claimed that the woman that they were guiding was Marilyn Monroe. These guides were Bee, Arnold, Douglas, and Tom Campbell; Basil Colford; George, Lawrence, Leonard, Weaver, and Robert Hennessy; Amos, Derwood, Richard, and Nelson Jardine; Bill and Junior Mersereau; Lloyd Sturgeon; Bill and Martin Vickers; Ephraim Keenan; the Washburns, Bob, Dennis, and John; and Francis Vickers, a cook and the top community butcher. The daughters of the river also came and chewed the one-cent bubble gum, played the jukebox, and joined in the songs: the Campbell, Jardine, Hennessy, Hallihan, Keenan, and Vickers girls. Sometimes the guides would walk these young women home.

Lloyd Sturgeon, who had just returned from the Yukon, revealed one evening that, if you wanted to get a big price for a section of river that was no more than a chub hole, you should always sell it on a windy day (an upriver wind, preferably). Then your buyer couldn't tell if the water was running fast or slow, but he would know that fast water holds salmon. And if you had a friend to send to the alleged pool ahead of you with a fishing rod and two dead grilse, the pool would likely go that day and for big money. John Washburn told of being storm-stuck up Cains River in three feet of new snow without snowshoes. He had to improvise by strapping a frozen codfish to each foot. Using the fish as snowshoes, he was able to walk out of the woods on top of the snow. "I came out of the woods and down the river ice, no trouble," he said. "When I got home, Father asked, 'How'd ya get out, John?' 'I came C.O.D.,' I said."

Father has now retired from active outfitting, guiding, storekeeping, and woods work. He and Mother live in the family farmhouse and love to reminisce about the days when this little community was more active — when father circulated petitions for the region's first hydro and telephone lines, as well as when the new Howard Road, which brought new growth to the area, was built in 1947.

I think of all this now in the semidarkness of early morning as poplar leaves scatter and blow into the river, submerge, and drift away in water that overnight has turned from crystal to burnt cylinder oil. Today will be our traditional Thanksgiving at the old cabin. We have watched the wild geese go south again. Last evening we counted thirty-seven flying in a V southwest up the river. "Thirty-seven Thanksgiving dinners," father said. Now eighty-five, he says all we can pray for is to live to see them return in the spring, but I have heard him say this a good many times. Outside I can hear the slamming of doors and the bark of voices as my sons, now men in their twenties, start their pickup trucks. Today they are going to guide at the Old River and the Black Rapids Lodges, which are near home. But they will make it back for the meal and will bring their girlfriends with them. As their rattling old trucks motor out the lane and gather speed in opposite directions on the chip-seal highway, I think of Norman Maclean's famous words, "We are a family forever haunted by waters."

Guides' Talk

"Is your guest having a good vacation so far?"

"I think so."

"She seemed a little subdued this morning, that's all."

"Well, she's going home tomorrow with only one small fish."

"Holidays never really measure up to expectations, though, do they?"

"I guess not. Fact is never really a match for the glories of a good imagination."

"Except when it's looked back at, from down the road, and the more time that passes, the better it will look."

"But only if it's a good time. If a good feeling is planted, a good feeling will grow."

"So we have to cheer her up so she doesn't turn sour on us all."

"She seems to have pretty good resilience, so far."

"I know. If we can keep her happy for one more day, next winter all of this will have been much more exciting."

"For us, too, but I know, it doesn't matter about you and me."

"That little fish she caught will have grown to maybe a ten-pounder, and the fight it gave her will stretch to twenty minutes, and you and I will have become better guides, and the camp will have had better beds and better food and . . ."

"That's why we have to keep her happy. How she remembers us will depend on the state of mind she's in while she's here. If she gets a bad taste, it will sour the whole thing forever. And you cannot swing it around afterwards once it's in the mind that way."

Wayne Curtis

Vincent Swazey

Frederick Vincent Swazey was born July 27, 1933, in Boiestown, the son of a fishing and hunting outfitter. He is married to Hazel Price and they have two daughters, Michelle and Andrea.

Vin began fishing for trout at the age of five along with his father, Fred, and his older brother, Lawrence. In characteristic tall-tale fashion, Vin would say that having mastered trout fishing within a couple of days, he thought he should take on a bigger challenge and start fishing salmon. He remembers tying flies using the only material available to him in those days: chicken feathers from his father's hens, coloured chewing-gum wrapping, and bits of Christmas tree tinsel to add a little flash. Adept at the art of handling a canoe, Vin was already going fishing along with his father's guests, ferrying them across the river to the island pools, by the ripe old age of nine.

Vin began his formal guiding career before the days of outboard motors, when guests would be poled by canoe from pool to pool. Indeed, he has made the trip from Half Moon to Boiestown and even on to Renous at the head of the tide numerous times. Vin is one of a handful of dedicated and experienced guides still working who can guide a guest completely by canoe the entire length of the Miramichi in all water conditions.

Vin has spent most of his life as a guide and camp manager. He managed Camp Baldi on the Bonaventure River, Quebec, back in the seventies and Camp Russell in Ludlow, New Brunswick, both then owned by the Pittston Corporation. More recently Vin managed Camp Thomas Salmon Club in Blackville, owned at the time by Ingersoll-Rand. Besides this, he continued to operate Tuckaway Lodge in Boiestown, which was built in 1939 by his father.

Over the years, Vin has entertained many Canadian and American anglers as well as the occasional guest from England, Ireland, and as far away as Japan. Regular guests at Tuckaway Lodge are Mr. and Mrs. John Fraser. Mr. Fraser was Speaker of the House of Commons in Brian Mulroney's Progressive Conservative government.

For many guests the highlight of the trip to Tuckaway is the upriver canoe trip. Guides and guests put their canoes in at Burnt Hill or Half Moon and canoe out to the lodge. Sometimes this trip is made twelve times in the run of a summer. "The water is very fast up in there, places like The Narrows or Big and Little Louie," says Vin, "We have to be very careful." Vince has only gotten wet once or twice in thirty-five years of canoeing. "In the old days you didn't dare fall out of a boat. The old people would make fun of you if you let that happen. But one time, crossing the river with my brother Lawrence, the pole got caught in the rocks, and this pulled me off balance so I had to jump into the water, which was about four feet deep. It was summertime so it didn't make too much difference."

Entertaining is certainly an apt description for Vin's approach to keeping the mood upbeat among his guests during the inevitable lulls in the action. An incident he still laughs about occurred during one spring season. Always looking fashionable and photogenic in case he might be caught in an action shot, Vin was wearing a Crocodile Dundee-style hat. A guest commented on Vin's headwear and asked if he would lasso a salmon. Never one to turn down a challenge, Vin reeled in some of the line which he had been trolling behind the boat and made one of his long expert casts. He soon felt the line tighten. Already amazed, the guest was absolutely incredulous when the fish was in the net and it was evident that it had a half-hitch around its tail! When the guest blurted that he didn't believe his eyes, the equally astounded Vin nonchalantly asked, "What is it going to take to make a believer out of you?"

Vin has a seemingly endless supply of amusing stories from his years on the river. He becomes very serious, however, when the discussion turns to the plight of the Atlantic salmon. He has seen from personal experience the serious decline in trout and salmon stocks returning to the Miramichi each year as a result of a few decades of over-fishing, heavy poaching, and changes in the river's watershed. Vin has responded to the challenge by becoming actively involved in numerous organizations and committees devoted to the conservation and enhancement of the Atlantic salmon and its habitat. He has been a member of the Miramichi Salmon Association since 1965. Currently he serves as a senior vice-president of this well-known and worthwhile organization. Vin also serves on the executive of the Miramichi Watershed Committee and is a director of the Registered Outfitter's Organization of New Brunswick.

A knowledgeable and helpful guide enhances the image of salmon angling to visitors and helps to promote an appreciation of this tremendous natural resource. An outfitter and guide himself, Vin seeks to improve the awareness and quality of service offered by others in the area. Toward this end, Vin has instructed guides in courses offered by the New Brunswick Community College.

Vin Swazey's accomplishments to date have already earned him a spot in the Fishing Hall of Fame at Doaktown's Atlantic Salmon Museum. He has also been included on the honour roll of the Atlantic Salmon Federation for his efforts as a respected ambassador for the conservation of *Salmo salar*. A youthful demeanour, his love for his cause, and the sparkle in his eyes suggest, however, that Vin Swazey might be just getting started.

Guide's Talk

"George, you guided up at The Popples one time, didn't you?"

"Yes, we guided for black salmon, me and my brother Clarence and Joey Cain."

"Joey hooked a big beaver one day when he had almost all his line out. When it slapped its tail the sport said, 'That's a big salmon.' 'I know it is,' Joey said, even though when he saw the splash he knew it was a beaver."

"I knew Joey. We used to box."

"He was a good boxer but he took it to the streets."

"He was quite a character.

"Poor Joey always carried a bottle of wine with him in the boat. He would sip wine and rave about the sun and the trees and the fish being gods. One day when he was cranking the motor, he dropped his bottle in the river. 'What was that you dropped?' the old sport asked. 'That's primer,' Joey said, 'primer for the motor.'"

Wayne Curtis

Renate Bullock

Renate Bullock was born in Germany and immigrated to Canada as a child in 1953 along with her parents and an older brother. She grew up and was educated in Saint John, New Brunswick. At an early age she showed a keen interest in the outdoors. A special affection for horses developed during her teen years, and she actively participated in harness racing. That is where she met her husband, Fred Bullock, a Saint John dentist.

Renate was introduced to fly-fishing in 1966 while honeymooning with Fred at Rocky Bend, a famous salmon pool on the Main Southwest Miramichi. In 1973, the Bullocks purchased a camp near Boiestown. Here Renate became addicted to salmon fishing, and she fished at every opportunity, getting tips and guidance from friends. Her affinity for the sport was apparent. Renate had an intense desire to excel, and she caught her share of salmon regardless of conditions. Renate obtained her guide's licence in 1977. She intended to guide family members from out of province when they came home for their annual visits. Her experience afield grew while she honed her fishing skills and learned the basics of fly-tying. Her professional guiding career started in 1986 when a neighbour, Vin Swazey, who operates Tuckaway Lodge, approached her to lease her salmon pool for his guests. Thus a guiding position was negotiated.

Renate recalls, "A lesson I learned that first year was to never say no when asked if an unlikely-looking fly would catch fish." She had been working with a Nova Scotian on his first salmon trip. It was August, and the water was low. "He showed me his flies, which were large black salmon streamers. He wondered if these could be used for the bright fish. I told him that we use this kind of hook in the high water of April or May, but that they'd never work in this low water on these discriminating bright salmon. The Nova Scotian also asked head guide Vin Swazey the same question and was told the same thing. 'No, they're spring flies,' Vin said. There were fish in the pools, but they wouldn't rise for the choice flies recommended by the guides. After several days of futile attempts to raise a fish, the guest decided on his own to tie on one of the streamers. In no time he had hooked three fish, and I was scrambling through my fly box. I found my only streamer, one of my own creations called a Guiding Lady, which we started using. It produced action that afternoon as well. The Nova Scotian, of course, still returns to the Miramichi annually and looks up his favourite guiding lady."

Though Renate had long been familiar with the various wet and dry flies which are traditional patterns in the area, that incident helped to spark a new interest in fly-tying. She experimented with various patterns and sizes in hard fishing. Her willingness to "go the extra mile" had gained respect from even her most experienced fishing guests, who at first may have been wary of fishing with a woman guide. Today this no longer seems an impediment; many of the sports request Renate as their guide.

Renate has a love for all wildlife, so hook-and-release salmon angling is a natural instinct for her. She is proud to be the first woman to become a life member of the Miramichi Salmon Association. She also has a membership in the Atlantic Salmon Federation. She believes her daily example on the river will in some way contribute to sustaining this wonderful species.

She has a vested interest in the environment and in the future. Renate is the mother of three sons: Frederick, Jr., James, and Daniel. Dan, in particular, has inherited some of his mother's fishing genes. In 1992, he spent several months in Russia as an Atlantic salmon guide on the great Ponoy River — another reason why Renate believes we must strive to protect *Salmo salar*, our international goodwill ambassador.

Guides' Talk

"Boys, is Buzz coming up to guide this fall, I wonder?"

"I don't know for sure. Someone said he was coming if he didn't lose his guide's pin in that racket he got into with the wardens."

"That's right, too. They caught him drunk with a few salmon last summer."

"You know Buzz. When he has a drink or two he just can't seem to leave the fish alone."

"The greatest little lad in the world, too. And some kind of a guide. If he doesn't come, we're all sure gonna miss him."

"The boss is going to miss him. Who else can he get that knows this water?"

"What about Fitz?"

"Fitz said he'd come if it was a little longer route. But he just got the welfare coming and he doesn't want to screw that up for three weeks' guiding."

"And I don't suppose they'd pay him under the table."

"No no, they wouldn't do that."

Philip Lee

146

Bill MacKay with guest Jenny Pratt.

Bill MacKay

Bill MacKay is probably the best canoeman in Canada. He has spent a lifetime on the river as a guide, and this requires skill, but he has also won more than one hundred canoe races in Canadian competitions. He has a room full of trophies, award certificates, ribbons, and medals to commemorate his many achievements on the water.

Bill MacKay was born in 1932 in Hayesville, and he started guiding in 1950. He has guided for outfitters such as Salmon Brook Camp, Clayton Stanley Stewart's, Pond's Resort, Griffin's Inn, and Rocky Brook Camp, where he has worked for the past twenty-seven years.

Rocky Brook Camp is located along the uppermost reaches of the Miramichi at the mouth of Rocky Brook Stream. It was owned for years by the Miramichi Lumber Company but is now owned by Avenor. There is a staff of nine guides, who are employed for twenty-five weeks from early May to the end of September, when the fishing season ends on this part of the river. Bill MacKay is the senior man and guide foreman. Fellow guides at Rocky Brook Camp are Hardy MacKay, Spencer Price, Warren Price, Allen Munn, Barry Munn, Bradley Storey, Tom Lovelace and Brian Spencer. Camp manager is Manley Price of Boiestown.

Through the years, this great fishing lodge has hosted such famous guests as Jane Powell, Dickie Moore, David Rockefeller, A.B. Dick, Roger Smith, Benny Goodman, Bing Crosby, and Prince Charles. There were also a host of less known anglers such as the owners of the Toronto Blue Jays, business tycoons, judges, and physicians.

At Rocky Brook Camp, the guests fish Rocky Brook Stream and Clear Water Stream and pools with names like Upper and Lower Sisters, Graham's, Salmon Rock, Home Pool, Colter's Run, Old Stove, and McClosky's. Many of these pools can be fished by wading, as the river is small up here and a good caster can reach almost anywhere. However, many guests prefer to make river runs. A favourite canoe trip is from Half Moon to Norrad's Bridge in Hayesville, which is a forty-seven mile stretch of turbulent water. Some of the rapids in this run have to be portaged around, especially when the water is high. The dangerous whitewater pools in high water are Push and Be Damned, Big and Little Louis, The Narrows, Peter and Paul, and Burnt Hill.

Bill has seen many people capsize in his forty-five years in these waters. He has saved the lives of fellow guides and guests, and he has also arrived on the scene when it was too late and a search for a body was undertaken. He once capsized in a pool called Two Mile and a

Half Pond and lost a new rifle. Later he canoed the rapids again with a metal detector, this time dragging an anchor to slow down the boat. He found the rifle.

One of Bill's partners in canoe competition is Mervin Green, who is head guide at a neighbouring outfit, the Salmon Brook Fishing Club. Mervin and Bill have won many canoe races in this province as well as Nova Scotia and PEI. They won fourteen canoe races in one summer. These two men won the 1959 Miramichi River race from Doaktown to Blackville, beating out the Brophy brothers, Pat and John, for first place. Now Bill MacKay canoes with his daughter, Tammy, and together they have won several races.

Some of the best years for fishing at the Rocky Brook Camp were from 1969 to 1972. In each of these seasons the camp pools gave up over a thousand fish to anglers. The

Jenny Pratt with guide Bill MacKay.

camp record at Rocky Brook is a twenty-eight-pound eleven-ounce salmon which was caught by Don Jenkins at Salmon Rock Pool in the month of August.

Over the years, Bill has been witness to some unusual occurrences. Once he saw two anglers hook the same fish at the same time, and each went to the opposite side of the river to play it. On one occasion he has scooped the wrong fish, a wild salmon that happened to be swimming through a narrow channel near the one that was hooked.

Bill has been in charge of canoe runs with scouts and boys' clubs and church groups. And he has been baptized a few times himself, perhaps using a few biblical words in the wrong fashion. He has canoed the river hunting ducks for the government, and, on one occasion when his truck broke down near Half Moon, he carried his canoe several miles to the river and paddled home. "There was no other way I could get out!" he says.

On one December day, Bill lay on the board ice and grabbed a live salmon which was lying in the shallows. (Board ice occurs along the river in early winter when the eddies are the first to freeze over.) He carefully reached down and grabbed the big fish by the tail and snapped it onto the ice beside him. It was a very cold day, and the fish froze into a semicircle instantly. He took the fish home and left it in the outside kitchen, where it stayed frozen for days. A week later, his mother said, "Bill, bring in that salmon you caught, so we can clean it for supper." Says Bill, "I brought the salmon into the warm kitchen. When the fish began to thaw, it came to life and kicked onto the floor. I had to kill the fish again!"

Once a neighbour and fellow river man Raymond Munn (who for many years was a federal warden) told Bill he had hooked a forty-pound salmon not far from their home on the main river at Hayesville. Not believing Raymond, Bill countered with the old story of hooking a lantern that had been lost on the bottom of the river for years. "The lantern was still burning," he told Raymond, who did not believe *this* story. Said Bill to Raymond, "If you will take fifteen pounds off your fish, I'll blow out my lantern!"

Guides' Talk

"Boys, where would a lad go ta get a fish this evenin'?"

"That's a good question. Has anyone tried the Gray?"

"Water's still too high for there."

"What about the Ledges?"

"Good as any. I'll take 'im there."

"You never know, he just might hook something. I was talking to your lad this morning. Seems like a nice fella. Been fishing a few years, too."

"Yeah. A coupla years ago he was here in real good fishing and he caught a few. Now he won't listen to a thing I tell him. His leader's too short and he's using them big flies in this low water. And when you tell him to put on a longer and a smaller leader or to change to a small hook, all he says is, 'This is what I caught fish on last year.'"

"In that case just let him flail the water. But he likely won't catch anything."

"And he starts right off with a long cast, every inch he can throw, and he stays with the big cast all day. Even in them narrow channels that he could fish with ten feet of line."

"If he did hook a fish on a long cast like that, he'd never land it. It's hard to get a set on a fish with big long cast. But, as you say, you can't talk to him. So just let him flail the water."

"All he thinks about is the long cast. And the double haul, and the tight loop, and all that crap. He learned it all in some course in the States."

"I know. I'd rather have someone who never had a rod in his hands before. You can start him off with just the leader and let him work his way out. And he'll get as much."

"More. Most a these fellas are fishing way out past the fish. I saw one jump right at the end of his rod this morning."

"I know. He was waded out to the top of his waders, too."

"Standing right where the fish lay."

"I told him just to wade to his knees."

"But he kept working his way out. Reaching toward the other shore."

"And the big long cast . . . "

"Now, I'd sooner fish with a beginner any day. At least he'll listen to what you tell him."

Mervin Green

Mervin Green was born in 1934 in Saskatchewan, where his parents had moved during the Depression. The family returned to the Miramichi in 1936, and Mervin grew up in Hayesville, where he and his wife Myrna still live. He had gone back to the prairies when he was in his mid-teens but was disappointed by the flatness and lack of water. After a stint in Ontario, Mervin returned to the Miramichi and settled in Hayesville. At the age of seventeen, he began his career as a river guide.

His first boss was Murray Calhoun, who operated the Salmon Brook Camp, an outfit built in 1929 near Hayesville. Mervin worked his way into the position of camp manager, a job he still holds. Mervin is now also a part owner of this club, along with Austin Buck, Bob DeVilbiss, Brook White, and Palmer Baker. At Salmon

Brook, parties of four are looked after by seven people. Each angler has a guide of his or her own, and there is a cook, Valerie Fardy, and a cookee, Izella Reed. Fellow guides at Salmon Brook Camp are Arthur Lovelace, Herb Munn, Charlie Munn, and Clarence MacKay.

Later, Mervin acquired the additional job of managing the Dead Man Fishing Camp, an outfit forty miles upriver from Hayesville. The lodge was originally built in 1929 by Mr. Charles Adams (who had purchased the Boston Bruins and Boston Gardens in November, 1924), but it was sold to a Mr. Densenso, who in turn sold to Peter and Jack Schultz of Pennsylvania in 1950. Mervin rebuilt the camp in 1966. To build this hundred-and-ten-foot-long cabin, Green stumpaged and cut logs from the hills well upriver from Dead Man and rafted them down to the campsite. So secluded is the location that cement for the camp's foundation had to be mixed in an old washtub with shore gravel and carried to the site in buckets.

The Dead Man Camp has four miles of fishing water between Burnt Hill and Clear Water. Situated seven miles above Rocky Brook, this outfit is without telephone service or electric power. The lights and appliances are operated by a generator.

Dead Man was given its name during the log-driving days, when there was a portaging depot there. Evidence of the log landing sites can still be seen, with their second-growth steep hillsides overlooking the frothing Miramichi. In this area the Miramichi River is probably its most spectacular. There are miles of whitewater, ledge, and boulders that have claimed many lives through the years. During the depot days, a man was hired to live there and look after the storehouses. One old Irishman, after years at the depot, was found dead in his bed by lumbermen who thought he was asleep. They grabbed his beard and gave it a tug to wake him. When his beard came off they knew the man had been dead for weeks. Another version of the tale from Dead Man Camp is that the old fellow had fallen under his sled, which was loaded with logs, and his oxen had pulled the load over him.

Mervin has guided in these rough waters all of his adult life. The collection of trophies that fills one side of his living room shows that he is one of the best canoeists in Canada. He has also won over a dozen races in the Maritimes, and he is one of the few men to have canoed all the way across Canada. His journey, which he made as New Brunswick's representative in the Centennial celebrations, took him one hundred and four days of paddling between May 24 and September 4, 1967. His canoe came in fifth.

Some of the best fishing that Mervin can remember was in 1968 at Dead Man Camp when, after sixteen days in September, four rods had landed one hundred and fifty-six fish. Twenty of these were big salmon; the rest were grilse. Green's biggest fish was thirty-eight pounds, caught on June 17 one year in the 1980s.

Mervin and Myrna Green with Leslie and Merlin Palmer.

Mervin has guided American senators and governors, counts from Britain, and heads of state from home, including Roland Mitchener when he was Canada's Governor General. Guiding with Mervin at the Dead Man Fishing Camp are Bobby, Harry, and Regina Norrad; Vince and Wilbur Munn; and David Green.

Mervin Green is one of the best storytellers on the Miramichi, as well as a practical joker. He related to me an incident that I now believe is true. An old man had died during a hunting expedition at a secluded cabin away upriver from Boiestown. Clayton Stanley Stewart, a fellow guide, had approached Mervin to go with him to the remote camp to bring the dead man's remains out by canoe. This was at the request of the RCMP, who didn't know the river, or where the camp was, or that it could be reached only by canoe. Mervin agreed to go, and, with a body bag and a stretcher, he and Stewart drove to the uppermost location accessible by four-wheel-drive and portaged to the cabin. Here they found the Mounties waiting for them with another body bag and a stretcher of their own, and they loaded the corpse into a bag and set off down the river.

Halfway to the settlement, more Mounties were waiting on the shore. Having found an access route to the river, they decided to take the dead man on by power wagon. Stewart went with the Mounties, leaving Green to bring out the canoe.

Mervin paddled alone for several miles and finally, after rounding a sharp bend, came upon a friend who had been deer hunting. Mervin offered to give him a ride to the settlement. During the course of this journey, because they had a body bag and stretcher in the boat, the men decided they would play a practical joke on the folks who were waiting for the remains to arrive in the community. Mervin's friend got in the body bag, which was then zippered up so that only his boots were visible. He then lay on the stretcher to be paddled into Boiestown where a group of curious people waited at the shore.

Says Mervin, "When they saw me coming with the body, some of the women in the group started to cry, others praised me for my courage and calmness in the presence of a dead man. When I shouted for a neighbour to come and give me a lift, he said he couldn't if his life depended on it. 'I can smell him from up here,' he shouted from the bank, and he commenced to vomit . 'Well, I can't carry him alone,' I said. 'That's a big hill. Maybe I'll see if I can make the old son of a whore walk!' I stood the body bag up and kicked my friend behind the knee, and he started walking, stiff-legged, like. At this, one of the women screamed and fainted on the shore. 'Now he's gonna get ya!' I said to the neighbour, but he was running by then, into the woods. I didn't see him again for a long time."

Guides' Talk

"Boys, what are yas workin at?"

"Guiding right now . . . down for George."

"What kind of a river is it down there?"

"Rocky and fast, take the canoe pole right out of your hand."

"I know, a salmon would have to hang on to the bushes to get up through. But great water to hold fish, they say."

"Oh, great water, even in the warm part of the summer, August. If a man couldn't get a fish down there he should quit fishin'. Did ya ever guide yourself, Tom?"

"Guide? Guide, cripes yes. I guided for Allen's back in the forties for a dollar and a half a day, poling a hateful old sport way ta cripes up Cains River, and it snowin' and rainin', and fishin' down."

"How far up would ya pole?"

"Oh, we'd pole way ta cripes up to the mouth of Sabbies."

"That's a long pole."

"A long pole, yes."

"I never knew you guided."

"Oh, yes, boys, I guided there for a good many springs. One day I remember poling up to Sabbies. It was in 1949. I poled way ta cripes up there, and we just got started to fish when I saw a smoke down at the mouth of Cains. I wanted to leave right then, but I couldn't. So we fished our way down, and when I got out, my old home had burned. Just a little smoke coming up among the trees was all that was left of the ol' place. We lost everything. Oh, yes, boys, I guided quite a few springs there for Allen's."

Clayton Arthur Stewart

As a youngster, Clayton Arthur Stewart worked the log drives on rivers
including the Bartholomew, the Cains, the Dungarvon, and the Main
Miramichi. Born in Quarryville in 1924, he started his guiding career
with Campbell's Fishing Camps in Upper Blackville in 1949. He worked
for Campbell for several years, guiding at outfits on the main stem
Miramichi and the Cains. "In those days we were allowed to keep six
fish a day and some days we would have our limit by ten o'clock in the

morning. Sometime two or three fish would rise to a single cast," says Clayton. "I remember hooking a salmon on my back cast once when I was wading deep, and the flyhook happened to strike the water behind me."

Herman Campbell, according to Clayton, was one of the most knowledgeable men in the industry when it came to catching salmon. "He could set in the kitchen in a rocking chair and tell you where to go at any time to catch a fish and what fly to use. He was like Wallace Doak in that way, he seemed to know where a salmon could be expected to be caught, and he most always was right. He had great river sense."

For over thirty years, Clayton has been guiding for the Old River Lodge, near the home on the Hazeltown Road in Doaktown where he lives with his wife, Hilda. This outfit was first owned by a Mr. Bamford but was purchased by Alex and Vicki Mills in 1976. Among

Old River Lodge, owned and operated by Alex and Vicki Mills.

the many top-quality guests that Clayton has guided since going to work for Alex and Vicki Mills was Prime Minister Jean Chrétien. "This was back when Chrétien was finance minister for Pierre Trudeau. Chrétien had planned to stay a week, but after only one day of fishing, in which he got one salmon, he was called to an important meeting in Ottawa and had to leave in the middle of the afternoon. But he paid me for the full week's work and gave me a good tip," recalls Clayton. Another of Clayton's famous guests was jazz musician Hoagy Carmichael. A favourite guest is Pic Clay, a car dealer from Massachusetts, who has been coming to fish with Clayton for thirty consecutive years. This man caught the biggest fish of all the hundreds of guests Clayton has guided. It was a black salmon which weighed thirty-four pounds. Fellow guides at Old River Lodge are foreman Marty Stewart, Milford Arbeau, Floyd Weaver, and Jeff and Jason Curtis.

"One year we were fishing black salmon," recalls Clayton. "I believe it was 1973. Anyway, there were so many fish in the river that catching them became monotonous, and I took my guest and anchored my canoe in a bogan where I didn't think there would be anything but trout. But after only a few casts she hooked a twelve-pounder. The high water and ice jams had driven fish into backwaters everywhere. We got sick of catching them after a while."

"Trout fishermen are the hardest men to guide," says Clayton. "They won't listen to what you tell them. Mostly they are set in their ways and think that salmon can be caught in the same fashion as trout. But of course it's a whole different ball game. Trout fishermen and casting champions seem to think that the farther they wade and the longer they cast the better their chances are of catching a salmon. Which of course is seldom the case."

Guides' Talk

"See anything tonight, George?"

"Yeah, ol' timer. We had one on up there for a while, up on the bar there."

"Many fish showin' up there?"

"Yeah, we musta saw a hundred."

"And ya only hooked the one?"

"Yes sir! And it was foul hooked, too . . . by the fin. We were on that little island in the middle of the river. When he hooked the fish it just took off down stream crossways in that fast water. There was no way to hold it. The old lad was running out of line. I had to wade to shore and get the canoe, then come out and pick him up. We followed the fish downriver fast as we could, gathering up the line. It was played out, really, and nearly to shore when it flopped over the leader and broke it and then swam away with my butterfly trailing from the end of his dorsal fin."

"Well at least ya had him on for a while."

"Yeah, well, rotten leader, eh. You see any?"

"No, just a loon fishing under the water. It made a big wake here and there. We thought it was a salmon at first. The old lad changed flies three or four times."

"I hooked a loon once. Took a smelt streamer under the water, just like a fish. He stayed on for a bit and run around under the water as fast as any salmon. Then he came out of the water, and I thought I had a flying fish. Then he broke clear. The hook stayed in his feathers."

"Gives a new meaning to a feather-winged fly."

The Trout Hole Salmon Pool below Burnt Hill Brook.

Merlin Palmer

"There is no place on earth more exciting than Burnt Hill in the spring of the year," says Leslie Palmer. Leslie is the wife of Merlin Palmer, a river guide and canoeman for more than forty years on the upper reaches of the Miramichi.

Merlin Palmer was born in Bloomfield Ridge in 1938. He and Leslie, their two daughters and a son now live in a comfortable farmhouse in Parker Ridge.

Merlin started guiding in 1957. His first employer was Clayton Stanley Stewart, of Boiestown, who ran the Griffin's Inn, the outfit now known as the Burnt Hill Fishing Club. This is the oldest outfit of fishing camps on the Miramichi River. Located ten miles above Rocky Brook and twenty-five miles below Half Moon, it's the most upriver outfit on the Miramichi. The main lodge, which was built by a Mr. Jefferson in the 1800s, was originally cedar shingled, with verandas and gables. They called it the Old Fish House. There are many photos of the Old Fish House on the walls of Merlin and Leslie's home: big men in period costume standing with a day's catch of salmon strung on canoe poles between them. Jefferson sold the camps to Dr. Chase, a dentist from Fredericton, who in turn sold it to F.C. Dumaine in 1949. At this time, the old lodge was replaced by sprawling log cabins that may well be the

Author's collection

most attractive salmon lodge anywhere in eastern North America. Later, Mr. Dumaine sold to W.C. Bullock of Maine and Asa Allen of Florida. These men currently own the Burnt Hill Fishing Club.

Merlin Palmer (left) with F.C. Dumaine, a former owner of the Burnt Hill Fishing Club.

Merlin started looking after the Burnt Hill Fishing Club in 1974. He took over the outfit from Clayton Stanley Stewart, who retired to became a writer. As well as being head guide, Merlin is also the cook and caretaker. "I do pretty well everything, from plumbing and gathering firewood to buying groceries, serving meals, and taking the guests out fishing."

Here at the Burnt Hill Fishing Club, four guides look after six guests. There is not much canoeing as the water is too rough and the river is small enough that its pools can be reached almost anywhere by wading. The club owns one mile of prime river-front, and in this stretch of water there are seven salmon holding pools. One of these is the famous Trout Hole Pool. Another is the mouth of Burnt Hill Brook. Between early June and the end of September, in the 1960s and 1970s, these seven pools would have produced a high of eight hundred fish in a summer. "Catches have dropped off a bit, though, in the last few years," says Merlin. The modern record for this fishing club is a twenty-eight-pound salmon caught at Trout Hole one September in the 1980s.

Working at Burnt Hill with Merlin are guides Mont Norrad, Robert Palmer, and Charles Lovelace. Except for occasional days off, these men remain all season at the Burnt Hill camp.

Outdoor writer Lee Wulff fished here in the 1950s, guided by Merlin's dad, and he described the club as "among the best-equipped outfits and best holding pools I've witnessed in fresh water angling anywhere in the world."

The Burnt Hill Fishing Club hosted Malcolm Fraser, Prime Minister of Australia, in 1976. For his three-day visit, he brought with him a contingent of security people and two RCMP officers from Fredericton. This was all done in secret from the press. Another dignitary to come here, secretly and with his own security people, was the governor of Massachusetts.

The main lodge at Burnt Hill Fishing Club.

With its turbulent fast water, this end of the river has become a Mecca for canoeing enthusiasts. Leslie has counted over one hundred and fifty canoes going past on a single Sunday in May. This is rough water to canoe, and many times Merlin has been called upon to rescue amateur canoeists drifting past, clinging desperately to half-submerged boats after taking a spill in Trout Hole or Burnt Hill Brook rapids. It was in these waters that Dr. John Williamson of Fredericton drowned a few years ago. He had gone fishing alone on July 1. "The water was high," Merlin recalls. "Dr. Williamson had breakfast and went to the Lower Pitch to fish without a guide. He was gone for quite a while, but we didn't know he had drowned until someone saw his body adrift in the rapids three miles below the camp."

Through his forty years here as head guide, Merlin has seen many things happen, but none more unbelievable than an incident which occurred in the summer of 1995.

"On a June afternoon I went to the Trout Hole to fish, and I hooked and landed a twenty-two-pound salmon, which I released. Later in the afternoon, I hooked another large salmon in the same pool. This was a bigger fish that took out most of my line as it headed downstream in a fit of jumps and capers. Finally the salmon went around a rock in centre stream, and my line broke at the backing. I lost my new casting line and the fish. I went to the camp disgruntled, with the notion that I had given a whole new meaning to the phrase 'hook-and-release.' I had supper with Leslie and we played a game of auction forty-five as I told her about losing the big fish and my line. Later in the evening I took a canoe to go across the river to the spring for fresh drinking water. On the way across I looked on the bottom and saw my yellow casting line. I picked it up with the canoe pole, and sure enough the salmon was still on the hook. I yelled for Leslie to bring me the rod. Here, then, we threaded the line on, fixed it to the reel, and landed that big salmon!"

Guides' Talk

"She is a very pretty woman, and she throws a nice line."

"A nice line in more ways than one."

"She's a beautiful woman inside and out."

"A great conversationalist. That's for sure."

"But did you ever see anyone fish salmon that way?"

"No, who taught her?"

"God knows. She won't listen to anything I tell her."

"Did she ever get a fish?"

"I don't think so. Maybe last year when that big run was on."

"That's like a beginning golfer parring the course."

"Does she always cast upriver?"

"Yes. In a kind of roll cast. Mending she calls it."

"That's what they do for steelhead. I read that somewhere."

"She has a belly in the line. A salmon would never take that hook."

"I don't think she really cares. She's just enjoying the river."

Evelock Gilks

Evelock Gilks was born on a Blissfield farm in 1948, and the garden
hoe was his greatest boyhood enemy. To escape the strawberry fields
in the heat of summer, he would convince his father to let him go to
the river to get a fish for the table. "If I caught a salmon, he would let
me go again, and this became a kind of retreat from farm chores. I
always made sure I got fish one way or the other. It got me out of
the fields, so I learned to be a good fisherman at a very young age,"
Evelock says.

Evelock caught his first big salmon at a pool called Murray's Landing in 1958. Back then this was one of the best salmon pools on the Miramichi. "Later the government opened this water to the public, and the beautiful Murray's Landing was ruined for ever. We saw there and then how open water could ruin a pool."

Evelock started guiding in 1966 for Ralph Gilks, a relative who lived nearby and who was a small outfitter in the black salmon fishery. "I only worked there for a few years. I didn't care much for spring fishing. It was too dangerous." In 1972, he went to work guiding for Floyd Gaston at the Miramichi Salmon Club, which is located near Doaktown. When Floyd retired in 1987, Evelock took over as head guide, camp manager, and caretaker.

The Miramichi Salmon Club was originally built by a Mr. Hoyts, a wealthy Pennsylvanian who came here for his health in the 1930s, bringing his own servant and employing a number of local people as well. Later the outfit was bought out by Dr. MacDonald, a local medical doctor who ran it on a small scale. When MacDonald got old, the camp sat dormant through the fifties and sixties until it was purchased by the current owners, a group of businessmen, most of whom are Canadian. One of these men is Derek Oland, president of Moosehead Breweries. It is now run as a successful outfitting business, with Evelock Gilks in charge.

"We fish bright salmon only," said Evelock. "We keep twelve guests in camp from early June to early October. Most of these guests are here on three-day trips, so we go through quite a few fishermen in the run of a summer. We have three miles of river and ten private pools, and we have five main holding pools — Travis Bar, Brown's Bar, Mersereau, Little Pool and Wasson Bar — which we rotate among our guests. We fish two guests to a guide and two canoes to a pool in the rotation. In 1993 our guests caught over four hundred fish, but that dropped to about one hundred in 1995, which was the worst year that anyone on the river can remember."

Miramichi Salmon Club is mainly a hook-and-release fishing club.

"We also fish the Mill Brook Pool off and on. At this cold-water pool, even in the worst possible conditions, there are always three or four hundred fish holding."

Other guides at the Miramichi Salmon Club include Ed Brennan, Boyd Gilks, Leonard Storey, Marven Morehouse, and Colin Gilks, Evelock's son.

The biggest fish caught at Miramichi Salmon Club was a twenty-seven-pound Rocky Brook salmon caught one June 15 during the eighties by Evelock himself. This fish, which is over thirty-nine inches long, was mounted, and it now hangs on the wall in the main lodge of the club.

Through the years, Evelock has guided such important people as Yves Fortier, Canadian Ambassador to the United Nations under Brian Mulroney; John Fraser, when he was federal fisheries minister; Boston Red Sox superstar Ted Williams; and writer and film-maker Lee Wulff, who fished here with Williams, with Evelock as their guide.

"I saw two men hook the same fish at once." Evelock laughs. "They were fishing across from each other at Murray's Landing. It seems their lines got crossed, and the flyhooks caught together, and, when this happened, a salmon took the two hooks. The man on the north side of the river landed the fish because he was closest to shore. He cut the salmon in two right there on the shore and they each took half.

Miramichi Salmon Club.

"One time when I went down to the pool, a man from New York was wading around the shallows, and he had his high waders on backwards. They were on the wrong feet and somehow they were twisted so that the suspenders crisscrossed on his chest. He looked like he had gone through a wringer washer. I can still see the company's brand name, Red Ball, on the guy's backside. He had fished two hours that way. Didn't know the difference."

Through the years, Evelock has rescued four men from drowning. "I once saw a man slip on the ice that had formed in the bottom of his canoe on a cold day in April when we were fishing black salmon. He fell overboard and was clinging to his outboard motor. I started my motor, and, without pulling the anchor, I motored across the river and towed him to shore. He was almost dead when I got to him. Another time in high water a man trying to start his motor had braced his foot on the boat's stern board to pull the cord. The board broke away, and the motor came off and went into the river. The boat started to fill with water instantly. The guide and his sport both rushed to the bow end as fast as they could.

Derek Oland (left), president of Moosehead Breweries, and his guide, Evelock Gilks.

Luckily I was close enough to be able to pick them up. There wasn't much time to act in either case."

Gene Hill (left), contributing editor of Field and Stream, *and Wayne Curtis.*

Guiding Gene Hill

"The guide is everything," Gene Hill said to me. "You can have the very best of accommodations, good food, drinks, comfortable surroundings, good personalities, and excellent equipment, and you can be on a good stretch of salmon water and have good fishing conditions, but if you don't have a good guide, chances are you won't catch fish. A top quality guide knows the river bottom, where the fish hold, what fly to use, what speed and angle it should be fished and what time of day a given pool produces."

We were drinking tea at the Bluestone Pool on the Little South-west Miramichi. Gene was a guest of André Goodin at the Miramichi Inn, the largest outfitter on that beautiful river, and I was guiding for André. It was early October, and we had spent our fifth day on the river and had no fish. But conditions were tough. It had been a tough year.

Still, I was concerned. Others in the camp were catching salmon. But I had no new tricks to offer Mr. Hill, certainly none that he hadn't already tried in his sixty-odd years of fly-fishing.

"I don't know what to tell you, I have no new mythologies."

"What fly would you use right now if *you* were fishing here?" he asked finally.

"I'd put on an Ingles butterfly if it were me," I told him. "It's the best all-around fly on the river."

"Ah, hell, I don't like fishin' a goddamn butterfly," he snapped. "Is that the only flyhook you guys use on this river?"

"Suit yourself . . . fish whatever you want."

Salmon were jumping and rolling all around him that day, but none were rising to his fly. Finally he said, "What do you suppose they're rolling for, Wayne?"

"The butterfly!" We both laughed.

Later in the evening, back at camp, he scoffed at me when I said, "Look, Gene, you only have two days left to fish. You haven't caught anything so far. If you would like to go with a more experienced guide, I wouldn't be at all offended."

"I wouldn't think of it," he said. "I couldn't be happier." He grinned, popped a match, lit his big pipe, and blew the smoke over me. "You are as effective as you can be. Yet you are invisible a lot of the time. And that's how a good guide should be, especially working with an old coot like me who likes his solitude on the river and knows or should know these fish as well as anyone."

"But you have a reputation to uphold. The other guys in camp, they're catching fish!"

He only looked at me and grinned.

"Not to mention my reputation as a guide, " I said.

"I don't give a damn about any of that. Do you?"

"Not any more than it matters to the guest."

"Then relax."

Gene Hill is an outdoor writer, an angler, and a hunter who has spent a lifetime in the field or writing about experiences afield. A Harvard man who has seen his work published in a hundred magazines, he has written twelve books, and he has been contributing editor of *Field and Stream* for many years. He wears Scottish tweeds and smokes a straight-stem pipe like Mark Trail. Gene is skinny, almost frail, and he sports a greying mustache. His manner is not unlike the demeanour of some of the British I've guided. I have read his column "Hill Country" all my life, so I felt privileged to be working with him. But I also felt pressure — to make sure that this famous man who could make or break a fishing camp caught a salmon. Call it responsibility. My livelihood depends on my guests' happiness. I felt the same pressure during the summer of 1995, when I worked with other men famous in fishing circles: Stan Bogdan, who builds the famous Bogdan reels; Jim Lorenz, a former National Hockey League superstar who is now a colour commentator for the Buffalo Sabres; and Jim Rickoff, a famous American outdoor writer who knew Ernest Hemingway. All had caught fish and left camp happy.

Gene Hill, sixty-seven, now writes out of Oracle, Arizona. As well as fishing around the world, he has hunted quail and other game most of his life and is a legend in outdoor writing circles. His right arm has weakened slightly from his many years of shooting, and when I stand beside him in the stream, he rests it on my shoulder. He is not casting like he used to. Like my own, Gene's eyesight is not . . . well, we pass the leader back and forth in the twilight (I don't want to be responsible for the knots). The eight-pound-test tippet and the number twelve turned-down-eye flyhook have become undefined to the point that we exchange glasses. Eventually we use a magnifying glass that he fumbles through a hundred pockets to find. I tie on the fly for him. But neither of us cares; we have more on our minds than fish. It seems to me that if we're fishing at all, it's only because we're here, at this great pool on this great river. "You're on the Miramichi, you may as well fish," I tell him. He answers, "I'm going to . . . after a bit."

In the morning around nine-thirty, when we get to our designated pool, I build a fire on the rocky beach and make tea. We sweeten this with brandy and sip from tin mugs as Gene smokes his pipe and tells

stories from his many travels — about the great salmon rivers of Scotland, where his ancestors came from, and the gillies he has fished with, and the great lodges he has stayed in on the rivers Spey and Dee, as well as some less-famous lodges here in Canada and in his own country. Gene talked about the fishing pals he has

Gene Hill (left) and Stan Bogdan.

travelled with, fellow magazine writers Ed Zern, Jim Rickoff, Lee Wulff, Nick Lyons, Dana S. Lamb, and a hundred more I've never heard of. Gene tells me how he and Lee Wulff narrowly escaped disaster in the wilderness of Labrador when the plane they were flying ran low on fuel; how, on the northern Quebec tundra, he was forced to sleep on a rock in sub-zero temperatures with only a caribou hide over him after Zern assured him that the outfit they were going to supplied everything including top-grade sleeping bags; how, when he forgot to treat his gillie with a drink of scotch one rainy day on the Dee, he was refused a dry match to light his pipe: "The only thing I have that is dry, Mr. Hill, is the back of my throat."

"I have fished Florida," I tell him, not wanting to appear entirely a stay-at-home, "Sarasota, one March break when the kids were out of school."

"That's wonderful," he says. And I hope he doesn't ask me much about the trip. I can't remember, it's so long ago. We sip tea and I tell *him* stories of *this* river: how one fall in the fifties, when I was ten, my brothers and I caught a barrel of salmon on fly rods; how Andrew Buck, an English teenager I guided this June, landed a thirty-pound salmon at the mouth of Cains; of the ghost that pulls the rod out of your hand here at Bluestone in the evenings when the moon is full; and about the moose in rut that chased me into the river not a week before. I am astonished at how much we have in common: we were both skinny youngsters, had gone to one-room schools. We both love radio shows and have a passion for writing. It's as if I'd discovered a long-lost brother.

"Are you going to throw a line?"

"What's that?"

"Are you going to throw a line?"

"Later . . . when the sun comes over that ridge and lifts some of the fog."

"Okay."

"When the temperature rises and the foam evaporates."

I wade into the stream to where the current is fast and hold the thermometer in the water. "Five degrees."

"About forty-two," he says. "Soon be time."

We talk writing now and recite poetry. I renew his interest in Frost and Hardy. He renews mine in Dylan Thomas and William Butler Yeats. We share Hemingway in Spain, Fitzgerald on Long Island Sound, Margaret Atwood in Canada's northlands, Jane Smiley in Idaho, and Tim O'Brien first in Vietnam and then at Lake of the Woods.

I want to see this man catch a salmon.

"Are you going to try a cast or two?"

"Later."

He goes to the fire and pours tea. He wants to know about the woodcock. "Do you have a decent speckled trout run? Do you have wild turkeys? Is there a deer hunt ?" We exchange pieces of prose for tonight in camp, books we've written, endorsed — suddenly a bear bursts out of the woods behind us. It half-swims, half-wades across the river, then runs into the woods on the opposite side, shaking water from its fur.

"Maybe I will try a cast or two," Gene says.

"Butterfly?"

"No, a black bear-hair. Did you not see the omen?"

"I saw one roll in the fast water."

"I saw it, too."

Gene Hill makes a short, neat cast and hooks the salmon. He plays the fish, holds the rod high, struggles for footing on the rocks. I stand beside him. He has his pipe going, even now. The salmon capers and jumps twice before tiring and coming to the surface to be tailed — almost. But it rolls over the leader and the line goes slack.

"The goddamn leader broke!" Gene stuttered.

Silence. He fumbles with the tackle.

"Did it break at my knot, Gene?"

"Who cares?" he says, and I know that it's true: the worst thing that can happen to a guide has happened to me. But Gene Hill, a gentleman, won't confirm it.

"A wind knot," he says. "I should have checked it."

"I should have checked it."

"It was a releaser, anyway." He grins again. "It's all the same. Isn't it all the same to you? That fish was a good ten pounds."

"I guess so."

On the last day of Gene Hill's visit, it was very cold, and we didn't go to the river. We took photographs of each other and had André take ours standing under trees in front of the guides camp.

In the evening, he treated me to some eighteen-year-old scotch as we exchanged addresses and telephone numbers. He gave me his new book, *A Listening Walk*. He would be back next year and would ask André if I'd guide him again. Eventually we shook hands, and I left him sitting alone in his cabin with a magazine. He was puffing on his big pipe.

Index

A

Adams, Charles 154
Adams, Fred 114
Adams, Richard 114
Agila, David 19
Aires, Senator 88
Allen, Asa 164
Allen, W. Harry 14, 62
Allen's Fishing Camp 56, 62, 72
Anderson, Gary 115
Arbeau, Wilson 58
Armstrong, George E. 14
Atlantic Salmon Museum 13, 98
Avenor's Rocky Brook Camp 147, 148, 149

B

Babcock, Dewey 107
Baker, Palmer 153
Basco, Willie 73
Bashline, Jim 82
Bashline, Sylvia 82
Beak, Ed 40
Beaverbrook, Lord 88
Belanger, Jack 57

Belford, Lord 34
Beliveau, Jean 66
Bentley, William, Sir 102
Berenson, Red 66
Bergan, Murdock 63
Beternick, Al 132
Big Hole Fishing Camp 87, 88
Bill Hollowood's Camp 39
Black Brook Salmon Club 39, 124
Black Rapids Lodge 88, 109
Blackmore, Fred 120
Blackmore, Harry 119, 120
Blackmore, Rita (Holmes) 119
Blackmore's Fishing Camp 119, 120
Blakney, Allen 88
Bogdan, Stan 82, 175, 176
Boyd, Bill 36, 124, 125
Boyd, Thomas 34, 39, 41
Boyd, Tom 33
Boyd, William 34, 37
Boyd's Fishing Camp 62
Boyd's Fishing Lodge 34, 35, 36, 39, 40, 41, 62, 124, 131
Braithwaite, Henry 14

Brennan, Ed 171
Brennan, Joe 48
Brennan, Joseph 58
Brennan, Tom 48
Brophy, Christopher 48, 55, 58, 63
Brophy, Clyde 59
Brophy, Cynthia (Vickers) 53
Brophy, Emery 40
Brophy, Joe 48, 59, 63
Brophy, John 41, 47-50, 53, 54, 55, 58, 78, 149
Brophy, Joseph 48, 55, 58
Brophy, Melvin 55, 57, 58, 63
Brophy, Patrick 41, 48, 53-59, 57, 63, 149
Brown, Kingsbury 27, 124
Brown's 62
Buck, Andrew 177
Buck, Austin 153
Bullock, Daniel 145
Bullock, Fred 143
Bullock, Frederick, Jr. 145
Bullock, James 145
Bullock, Renate A., 143-145
Bullock, W.C. 164
Burke, Lawrence 48, 58, 63
Burnt Hill Fishing Club 148, 163, 164, 165
Butterfield, Lou 77

C

Cain, Clarence 141
Cain, George 141
Cain, Joey 141
Cains River Enterprises 48
Calhoun, Murray 153
Camp Baldi 138

Camp Russell 101, 138
Camp Thomas. *See* Boyd's Fishing Lodge
Camp Thomas Salmon Club 138
Campbell, Arnold 131, 134
Campbell, Bee 134
Campbell, Charlie 130
Campbell, Douglas 56, 134
Campbell, George 58, 73
Campbell, Herman 160
Campbell, Ralph 58
Campbell, Tom 134
Campbell's Fishing Camp 72, 76, 159
Canan, Roger 82, 83
Carmichael, Hoagy 160
Charles, Prince 148
Chivers, Howard 54, 55, 57
Chivers, Sandy 54
Choan, Richard 97
Chrétien, Jean 160
Clay, Pic 160
Coburn, Bob 90-91
Colford, Basil 134
Colford, Gary 18, 73
Colford, Jim 58, 59, 71-73
Colford, Joe 56
Colford, Peter 63
Colter, Ashley 35
Connors, Bill 40
Connors, Charlie 78, 123
Coughlan, George 33, 34, 41
Coughlan, Norm 34
Coughlan, Peter 78
Crawford, John 34
Crawford, Ralph 34
Crimmins, Charles 14
Crosby, Bing 148

Index

Curtis, Ab 78
Curtis, Ann (Applin) 132
Curtis, Arnold 34
Curtis, Barbara (Sullivan) 128
Curtis, Brycie (Coughlan) 128
Curtis, Daphne 128
Curtis, David 132
Curtis, Edna 29
Curtis, Eldon 48, 58
Curtis Fishing Camp 124
Curtis, Gary 131
Curtis, George 42, 88, 109
Curtis, Herb 129
Curtis, Jason 20, 161
Curtis, Jean 88, 109
Curtis, Jeff 161
Curtis, John 48, 58, 75, 78, 87, 127-135, 132
Curtis, Marshall 34
Curtis, Preston 40
Curtis, Rick 40
Curtis, Roy 27-30, 78
Curtis, Scott 73
Curtis, Thomas 128
Curtis, Wayne 21, 67, 173
Curtis, Will 87
Curtis, Winston 78, 127, 129

D

Davenport, Arthur 67
De Vilbiss, Bob 153
Dead Man Fishing Camp 154, 155
Dean Bar Lodge 125
DeFarrell, Charles 77
Dempsey, Jack 94
Deveau, Robert 102
Dick, A.B. 148

Doak, Wallace 133, 160
Doctors Island Club 27, 62, 76, 78, 124, 131
Dolan, Charlie 34, 78
Donovan, Hal 83
Doolittle, James, General 64
Dumaine, F.C. 164

E

Eagles, Louie 132
Easley, Press 75
Egan, David 132
Estey, Joe 86

F

Fardy, Valerie 154
Fekeshazy, Alex 107
Fisher, Red 28
Flick, Art 132
Foran, Clayton 81-83
Fortier, Yves 171
Fraser, John 138, 171
Fraser, Malcolm 165
Fraser, Scott 114
Furlong, Stan 58
Furlong, Stanley 48, 58, 63, 72, 73

G

Galler, Henry 132
Gallivan, Danny 67
Garrison, Everett 107
Gaston, Floyd 170
Gilks, Boyd 171
Gilks, Colin 171
Gilks, Evelock 169-172
Gilks, Hubert 40
Gilks, Ralph 170

Gill, Leslie 107
Gillespie, Jim 76
Gillespie, Max 76, 78, 107-108
Gillespie, Paul 78
Gillette, Thomas, Admiral 64, 72
Goldman, Charles 64
Goodin, André 65, 81, 82, 83, 173, 178
Goodin, Susan 83
Goodman, Benny 107, 148
Gordon, Jason 83
Green, David 155
Green, Fred 56
Green, Mervin 149, 153-156
Green, Myrna 153, 155
Griffin's Inn. *See* Burnt Hill Fishing Club

H

Hallihan, Hugh 34
Hallihan, Joe 48
Hamilton, Dr. John 134
Hanson, Al 132
Hare, Louis 87
Harris, Alvin 78
Harris, Doris 88
Harris, Eugene 85-89
Harris, Tom 78
Harvey, Doug 34
Headslip, William 107
Hennessy, George 58, 63, 72, 134
Hennessy, Lawrence 134
Hennessy, Leonard 58, 134
Hennessy, Robert 59, 134
Hennessy, George, Sr. 48
Hennessy, Weaver 134
Hill, Curt 82
Hill, Gene 82, 173, 173-178

Hollier, Ernest 63
Hollowood, Bill 39
Houston, James 95
Hubbard, David 83
Hubbard, George 75
Hunter, Dennis 104

I

Isztwan, Andrew 82
Isztwan, Boris 82
Isztwan, Orest 82, 109

J

Jack Sullivan's Camp 62
Jardine, Amos 134
Jardine, Arch 124
Jardine, Derwood 134
Jardine, Jack 33-37, 124
Jardine, Nelson 134
Jardine, Richard 134
Jardine, Silas 34
Jenkins, Don 149
Johnston, Guy 114
Jones, William 101

K

Keenan, Clark 131
Keenan, Ephraim 134
Kelly, Lila 40
Kerlee, Charles 107
Kerlee, Vivian 107

L

Lamb, Dana S. 176
Lassen, Grover 119
Layton, Stanley 55
Le Breton, Xavier 83
Lebans, Al 39, 44

Index

LeBlanc, Romeo 88
Long, Allen 94
Long, Ernest 93-98
Loomis, Gary 82
Lorentz, Jim 65-67, 82, 175
Lovelace, Arthur 154
Lovelace, Charles 165
Lovelace, Tom 148
Lynch, Charles 102
Lyons, Dow 40
Lyons, Nick 176

M

MacKay, Bill 147-150
MacKay, Clarence 154
MacKay, Hardy 148
MacKay, Tammy 149
Maclean, Norman 135
Manderville, Carl 33
Matchett, Art 40
Matchett, James 87
Matchett, Morrisey 87
Matchett, Weldon 87
McAllister, Earl 88
McCormick, Dorothy 59
McCormick, Malcolm 58, 73
McKiel Brook Camp 102, 105
McKinnon, Bill 57
McLaughlin, Francis 108
Mersereau, Bill 134
Mersereau, Junior 134
Mills, Alex 160
Mills, Vicki 160
Miramichi Anglers Club 101
Miramichi Gray Rapids Lodge 39
Miramichi Inn 81, 82, 83, 173
Miramichi Renous Club 39, 76, 124

Miramichi Salmon Club 76, 170, 171
Mitchener, Roland 155
Mitchum, Robert 95
Monroe, Marilyn 77, 78, 95, 134
Moore, Adam 14
Moore, Dickie 34, 148
Moose Call Lodge 102
Morehouse, Marven 171
Morgan, Jim, Rev. 129
Mountain Channel Salmon Club. See Boyd's Fishing Lodge
Mountain, Clarence 34, 78
Mountain, Dana 40
Mountain, Eldon 39
Mountain, Frank 76
Mountain, Jody 40
Mountain, Maude (Underhill) 39
Mountain, Percy 34, 39-44
Mountain, Ralph 34
Mountain, Roger 40
Mountain, Vearyl 40
Mountain, Willis 34
Mullen, Sonny 102
Mulroney, Brian 138, 171
Munn, Allen 148
Munn, Barry 148
Munn, Charlie 154
Munn, Gordon 75-78
Munn, Herb 154
Munn, Raymond 40, 150
Munn, Rod 102
Munn, Vince 155
Munn, Wilbur 155

N

Norrad, Bobby 155

Norrad, Ed 14
Norrad, Harry 155
Norrad, Mont 165
Norrad, Regina 155
Norton, Dale 120
Norton, Debbie 119-121
Nutbeam, Sarah 128, 129

O

O'Brien, J. Leonard 87, 88
O'Donnell, Eric 40
O'Hare, Paul 33, 76, 124, 125
Oland, Derek 170, 172
Oland, Victor 34
Old River Lodge 20, 160, 161
Orr, Bobby 66, 72

P

Page, Evans 132
Palmer, Leslie 155, 163, 164, 165, 166
Palmer, Merlin 155, 163-166
Palmer, Robert 165
Patterson, Senator 88
Pearson, Anne 49
Perkins, Niles 132
Peterson, Weldon 58
Pond, Bradley 102
Pond, Keith 102
Pond, Linda 102
Pond's Resort 94, 101, 102, 103, 147
Powell, Jane 148
Pratt, Jenny 147, 149
Price, Bev 93, 94
Price, Erdie 102
Price, Manley 148
Price, Spencer 148

Price, Warren 148
Pringle, Tom 14

Q

Queenie, Edgar 87, 88

R

Reed, Doug 82
Reed, Izella 154
Renshaw, Jean 97, 98
Richard, Maurice 34
Rickoff, Jim 82, 175, 176
Ritchie, Tom 132
Robichaud, Louis 34
Rockefeller, David 148
Rockefeller, Stillman 64
Rogers, Jimmie 134
Rosenberg, Scott 33
Ross, Ted 102
Routh, Dorothy 123, 125
Routh, Jack 124, 125
Russell Fishing Camp. See Pond's Resort
Russell, Jack 94

S

Salmon Brook Camp 149, 153, 154
Sansom, John E. 14
Schiffman, Arnold 97
Schultz, Jack 154
Schultz, Peter 154
Scott, Bill 40
Shaddick, Harvey 85
Shaeffer, Meade 107
Sharkey, Jack 28
Shaw, Dave 40

Index

Shirley Sturgeon's Bed and Break-
fast 39, 42
Silliker, Guy 113-115
Silliker, Shawn 83
Slipp, Arthur A. 14
Smith, Guy 40
Smith, Joe 133
Smith, Roger 43, 148
Sneed, Sam 34
Spencer, Brian 148
Stan Furlong 58
Stanley Furlong 72, 73
Stevenson, Herbert 33, 37
Stewart, Clayton Arthur 159-161
Stewart, Clayton Stanley 23-25,
147-155, 156, 163, 164
Stewart, Henry 19
Stewart, Hilda 160
Stewart, Jerry 83
Stewart, Pat 94
Stewart, Robert 97
Stewart, Roy 83
Storey, Bradley 148
Storey, Leonard 171
Sturgeon, Lloyd 58, 134
Sturgeon, Shirley 39, 42
Sullivan, Jack 62, 108
Swazey, Andrea 137
Swazey, Fred 137
Swazey, Hazel (Price) 137
Swazey, Lawrence 137, 139
Swazey, Michelle 137
Swazey, Vincent 101, 137-140,
144
Sweet, Glenn 33

T

Towers, John 88

Trudeau, Pierre 160
Tuckaway Lodge 138, 144
Tucker, Dick 40
Tunney, Gene 28

U

Uncle Tom's Cabin. *See* Boyd's
Fishing Lodge
Underhill, Alfred 76
Underwood, John 28
Upper Oxbow Outdoor Adven-
tures 120

V

Vickers, Ambrose 34
Vickers, Ben 34, 40
Vickers, Bill 134
Vickers, Francis 59, 63, 131, 134
Vickers, George 48, 58
Vickers, Helen 71
Vickers, Jack 58, 63
Vickers, Jim 48, 58, 63
Vickers, Martin 134
Vickers, Max 34, 78
Vickers, Rita 59
Vickers, Stafford 34, 78

W

Wade, Charlie 48, 53, 54, 55, 57,
58, 59, 61-64, 72, 76, 77,
131
Wade, Herb 62, 72
Wade's Fishing Camp 41, 48, 53,
54, 55, 56, 57, 58, 59, 61-
64, 72, 73, 76, 78, 124, 131
Ward, Perley 102
Warren, Edna 123
Warren, Mary 36, 37

Warren, Maude 37
Warren, Ralph 34, 123-125
Warren, Tom 39
Washburn, Alex 72, 131
Washburn, Bob 54, 134
Washburn, Dennis 34, 134
Washburn, John 34, 41, 42, 134
Waugh, Danny 101
Waugh, David 102
Waugh, Lloyd 101-105
Weaver, Floyd 161
Webb, Marie 16
Whalen, Pat 75, 76
White, Brook 153
Wild Cat Camp 98
Williams, Ted 27, 28, 29, 30, 36,
    66, 76, 171
Williamson, John, Dr. 165-166
Wilson, Keith 94, 98
Wilson, Tom 95
Wilson's Sporting Camp 62, 94,
    97
Wright, Keith 109
Wulff, Lee 34, 64, 165, 171, 176

Z

Zern, Ed 176